From Poverty to Prosperity

A Black Woman's Multi-Million-Dollar
Real Estate Success Story
and Strategies You Can Use

To Brenda,

Thanks for your support
and friendship.

Jannie Carter Williams

Jannie Carter Williams

Back cover photo of Jannie Williams
by Steve Herlihy Photography.

Cover Image: Vertigo3d, istockphoto.com

ISBN: 978-1-7375505-5-6

Edited by BizSuccessBooks.com
and Published by
Legacies & Memories, LLC
St. Augustine, Florida

Editor: E.L. Wilks
Part I was written by Jannie Carter Williams.
Part II was written by E.L. Wilks, BizSuccessBooks.com
and Legacies & Memories, LLC.
Cover Layout and Interior Layout: Capri Porter.

BizSuccessBooks.com
LegaciesandMemories.com

"Thrift and toil and saving are the highways to new hopes and new possibilities."

– W.E. B. DuBois
The Souls of Black Folk

Dedication

To my parents, *William and Luella Carter, who instilled in us the values of hard work, honesty and family unity. Thanks for never giving up on me.

To my daughters, Lisa Carter and Jamie Sawyer, for giving me honest responses laced with love. To my grandson, Jacob Carter Sawyer, I am hopeful that some tidbit in this book will resonate with you now and in the future. You will grow to realize that education is a privilege.

To my siblings – my life mates – thank you all for being my protectors, teachers, advisors and cheerleaders: Lucille Carter Seibert, Geraldine Carter Pitts, Alline Carter Greer, *Willie Mae Carter Graham, Rose Carter Ballard, William Carter, Jr., D.D.S., Dennis Charles Carter, M.D., Cleo Carter, M.D., and Kenneth Carter, M.D.

To my nieces and nephews – because you are our future and have incorporated the spirits of Granddaddy and Grandmama. Watching you grow is one of the joys of my life. Always remember that William and Luella Carter loved you deeply and would instruct me to dedicate this effort to you:

Michael Seibert, M.D.
Ronald Seibert
Pamela Pitts, J.D.
Anthony Pitts, M.D.

Abigail Greer Morales
Kimberly Greer Terrell
Albert Greer, III
Angela Harrison
Gail Graham Sharp
Carolyn McClain
Rachel Ballard Mehr, M.D.
Percy Ballard, M.D.
Mary Carter Robinson, D.D.S.
William Carter, III, D.D.S.
Dennis Carter, Jr.
Amanda Carter, M.D.
C. C. Carter, M.D.
Nicholas Carter
Ashley Carter, D.D.S.
Candace Carter, J.D.
Kenneth Carter, Jr.

---

*Deceased

Acknowledgments

The following people made significant contributions to my life:

Agenia Clark, Ph.D., my mentor and friend, has given sage advice and unwavering support for decades. Fredia Wadley, M.D., and Stephanie Bailey, M.D., who gave me the opportunity to work in public health administration. Lifelong Bridge Club members: Jeanette Crowder, *Gloria Lewis, *Vicki Jarrett, *Deloris Powell, Anne McNair, *Dollene Myles, Lucille Seibert, Betty Thompson, Erma Todd, *Julie Williams. Irish Jones Harris, cousin, who discovered the only known picture of me as a toddler. The image captures the poverty into which I was born. Joan Seigenthaler Miller, a supervisor and friend, who gave me a copy of Desiderata in the late 1970s. It provided a template for living a full and healthy life. Stan Romine, a supervisor and friend, offered invaluable advice about surviving the world of work and preparing financially for retirement years. Pamela Pitts, J.D., my niece and financial advisor. Special friends: Martha Bickley, James Brooks, Annette Carroll, Charles Clark, Haley Clark, Brenda Corbin, Ericka Dixie, Tamara Gauldin, J.D., John Johnson, Julia Jones, Tina Lester, Maria Guess Lewis, J. Louis Nance; Darryl Nettles, Ph.D., Eura Patterson, Joseph Perry, Ed.D., *Margaret Pharris, Theodora Pinnock, M.D., Van Pinnock, Jeffrey Powell, J.D., Kim Crowder Small, Wendy Thompson, J.D., Emily Walker, Hattie and Reginald Williams, T.J. Williams. Clients: Thanks to each real estate client who worked with me through the years. Though space does not allow me to list your names here, my appreciation to you is boundless.

---

*Deceased

Contents

Foreword

Ever since Jannie Carter Williams was a young girl growing up in an impoverished Black family with nine siblings, living and working on a Tennessee cotton farm, she vowed she would learn how to overcome poverty and never be poor again. As an adult, she did exactly that. And, she far exceeded even her own expectations.

With hard work, determination and persistence, and by overcoming obstacles and setbacks from some bad life choices and living during a nation's racist times in the 1950s, '60s and '70s, Jannie reached her childhood goal of becoming financially independent. Today, she has a multi-million-dollar real estate portfolio producing passive income.

The story of how she did it is inspiring. For anyone who has started from scratch or dreams of jumping off the treadmill of earning little money, Jannie's story not only gives hope, it includes real-world and real-life practical ideas. Business lessons and strategies she learned, and her appreciation for how her parents and other family members helped her along the way, may be useful to others who see real estate as a path to financial freedom.

But no matter a person's career choice or business inclinations, success strategies revolve around character, and attitude, and mental tenacity. Jannie's story shows what it's like digging out of life's darkest despairs, a prerequisite to adding joy in personal and family life before finding and traveling the path to financial success.

Part 1 of this book chronicles Jannie's personal story: childhood, her family's life, her college years, life as a young adult and in marriage with a family, her early years in the workplace, and some of the many years of her first professional career as a dental hygienist.

Part II details her business story as she made major changes in both her personal and professional life, becoming involved in real estate, and starting and growing her business as a real estate agent, then as a property owner and investor. Her method of working and the best business practices and strategies she put in place – many of which will be of interest to others in business – are featured in Part II.

E.L. Wilks
BizSuccessBooks.com
Legacies & Memories, LLC

Preface

I wrote this book for three reasons. First, it allows me to share with others the guideposts, behaviors and strategies that ultimately helped me arrive at a place of inner peace and financial independence. I hope what I've learned in business and life will be helpful to others on a similar path.

Second, this book records the time in America's history when public schools transitioned from separate and unequal to integrated. As a child and teenager, I lived it. I also offer a glimpse of a time in family life before birth control pills were widely used. My parents had none; they had ten children.

Lastly, I want this book to provide hope and encouragement to any person who makes mistakes and wants to correct course and move in another direction. In my teen and young adulthood, I was an emotional shipwreck. Because I was able to push away thoughts of suicide and ultimately find joy and success in life and business, perhaps others will realize they can do likewise.

From Poverty
to Prosperity

Part I

Chapter 1

A Humble Beginning

My family was poor when I was growing up on a small West Tennessee farm near the town of Halls. Reflecting on that time, the most remarkable thing to me was that Mom and Dad were able to manage expenses and needs with very little cash. They were able to provide for ten of us kids. They had lived through the Great Depression (1929 – 1941). We never went hungry. I don't know how they did it, but I do remember the first time I fully realized we were poor. It was one winter morning in 1959.

It was the usual procedure each morning that Mom would fix us breakfast and then she'd say, "Go get your lunch money from your Daddy." Our school lunches were 15 cents. He dispensed the lunch money to my sisters, brother and me in birth order from oldest to youngest. On this day, as he put his hands down deep in the pockets of his khaki pants, he had a very strained, stressed look on his face as if he was about to cry. He came up with a dime. He dug into another pocket and found a nickel. He gave those to Rose, my older sister. I was next in line.

So, there we were, three of us lined up in order of age: Rose eleven, I was nine and my brother, William Junior, was six. It seemed hard for Dad to find 15 cents for Rose. I started thinking, what about me? It took Dad what seemed like a long time to dig up Rose's lunch money. What if he doesn't have any more? What will I do? I remember that anxious feeling.

Before that day I hadn't really thought much about money. We always had enough food, we played with each other, we had a good time, and I just hadn't thought about money. But on that particular day, when his pockets were empty, Dad slowly walked back into his bedroom with his head lowered like he was trying to figure out what to do. The three of us looked sadly at each other wondering what we would do if he couldn't find lunch money for all of us. We three knew what Rose did not verbalize. If Junior and I had to take a homemade lunch to school, Rose would take one also. We shared our time, space and poverty.

A few minutes later, we heard Dad shaking what sounded like a piggy bank. He emerged from the bedroom with 15 cents for me and 15 cents for Junior. Dad always came through for us.

On that day, in those few minutes, I grew up a bit. I started thinking, "What if Dad hadn't had the piggy bank? What if he hadn't saved those coins?" I decided that day that I would figure out why some people had money and some did not. How did the money system work? I vowed to figure this out to help my parents and myself. I formed one goal that morning that has stuck with me during my life: I don't want to be poor. Being poor is stressful. I can see that scene as clearly as if it happened today. Before the "Dad running short on lunch money morning," it had not occurred to me that our family was very poor. I decided that morning that I would figure out a way to escape poverty.

I don't remember doing anything differently after I had this realization, although I probably paid a little more attention to Mom when she talked about the need to get an education. I think I listened at a deeper level. And although it didn't inform my immediate actions much, it stuck with me and made an impact on me.

Roots

My family has a long history of impoverishment, including both my paternal and maternal grandparents.

My paternal grandfather, Papa Anderson Charles Carter, was born a mulatto slave in July 1862 in King William County Virginia. He did not know which day in July. Papa's biological father was the plantation owner. His mother was the cook. He said his mother acted as if she hated him. Consequently, at the age of eighteen, Papa left Virginia forever.

Papa told my father that immediately after he ran away from the Virginia plantation, he lived with and worked for Quakers in Pennsylvania. Papa said the Quakers were nice to him but there were no black women to marry. So, he moved on to Kentucky where he worked on tobacco farms. Finally, Papa settled in West Tennessee after working as a dock hand on the Mississippi River. After laboring hard and pinching pennies, in 1904 he realized his dream of buying a small farm in rural Halls, Tennessee.

On April 3, 1916, my father, William Carter, was born to Janie Claybrooks and Anderson Carter. My father and my uncle, Anderson Carter, Jr., dropped out of elementary school to work and help their parents survive and hold on to the farm.

In 1939, my father married my mother, Luella Hudson. Together they started a family and helped work the family farm.

My mother's parents were Louis Hudson and Beulah Hudson. His family moved from Vicksburg, Mississippi, to Dyer County, Tennessee, near Dyersburg. My maternal grandmother was born in

Lauderdale County, Tennessee, which adjoins Dyer County.

I knew them when I was growing up, but we didn't see them often. We usually visited on Sundays at church, or after church. But most of the time we were working, and they were working. In the wintertime, when we didn't work so much, we might see them a little more or during the holidays, but we did not spend a lot of time with them. My maternal grandparents had nine kids. Grandfather Louis was stingy, and he didn't want other people coming to their house looking for candy or cookies. That's the kind of person he was.

They lived in a different part of rural Halls than we did. Grandfather Louis was a sharecropper on the Pugh Farm. Today, it's still a big, active farm. My grandfather lived there as long as he was able to work, and then he moved into public housing.

'Y'all Need to Be Busy'

Work was an important lesson I learned when I was young living on our dirt farm in Western Tennessee, near the town of Halls, about seventy miles north of Memphis. Mom, Dad and all of us kids worked. I remember as a child being in the garden with my Mom pulling weeds and helping her gather the corn, beans, potatoes and other vegetables. It was really a smart thing my mother did.

It was her way of babysitting: mom put us to work. Mom and Dad had this saying: "An idle mind is the devil's workshop." They justified their ability to keep us busy as, "We're helping God out here. Y'all need to be busy."

Helping Mom plant the garden was a learning experience. She constantly monitored my seed planting. She would say, "That's too close," or "You're getting them too far apart," or "Don't push them way down in the earth." Mom said if you push the seeds down too deep, the seeds may rot rather than sprout.

During the fall cotton picking season, Mom introduced even her toddlers to the world of work. She gave her youngest child a small metal lard bucket. I remember a red lard bucket with a metal handle on it. Mom told us to pull the cotton out of the bolls and put it in the bucket. That's how we learned to pick cotton. As a young child, I remember when Junior got his first lard bucket. He pulled out one piece of cotton at a time and put in his bucket. When bolls of cotton popped open, each boll held five long white fluffy pieces. The human hand with its curving flexible fingers was perfect for clearing the boll with one quick reach. Mom showed William Jr. how to get more than one piece of cotton each time he touched the cotton boll. She cheered when Junior got more than one. He liked the cheers, so he quickly learned to spread his little fingers into the cotton boll and remove the cotton. As I observed Junior, I understood how I learned to pick cotton even before I could remember the lessons. Mom was a genius at teaching us to work.

All Carter children over twelve had a full six-foot cotton sack that strapped over the shoulders. We picked cotton and threw it in the sack. Usually each person picked two rows, one row on each side. With the sack held over my back with a strap, I'd go up and down the rows. The most I picked in a day was about 310 pounds. Three hundred pounds per day was considered a great accomplishment. We had scales to weigh the cotton. My Dad wrote down what each person picked. That's how we knew who picked the most cotton. Then we would empty the contents of the sack into a trailer and pick some more cotton. We started early in the morning and picked until the sun was down. We stopped for a quick lunch, which usually consisted of bologna, liver cheese, crackers and/or pork and beans.

In September and October when the cotton was fluffy and plentiful, the cotton was picked out of the bolls. Then in the cold winter, whatever cotton had been left in the fields would be pulled. We would put on thick gloves, pull the whole boll off and put it in the sack that was attached to our back. Cotton pulling marked the end of the cotton season.

This was the 1950s and 1960s before mechanical cotton pickers were widely used. We were the cotton pickers.

The picking was not as difficult for me as cotton chopping because fall was cooler than summer. Chopping weeds in the cotton was grueling because of the extreme heat. Summer days are longer than fall days. Chopping was a harder day than picking. We looked for ways to make it bearable. Sometimes we would sing. Sometimes my Dad might tell ghost stories or my Mom would talk about what we could become – or life's possibilities. It's what we did in order to make it, to survive.

Field labor was a kind of family time – singing, teasing, talking while we were actually working. These were things many families probably did while sitting around the house in the evenings or on weekends. We incorporated a lot into our labor. I must admit that somehow our days of labor transformed into quality family time. We got to know each other. Because we siblings worked side-by-side, we bonded deeply. We got to know each other well and we learned we could rely on each other. We each came away from childhood feeling like we ought to do our part – to carry our row, to pick our portion of the pounds. We still feel that way.

I remember us singing while we worked. My mother would start a church song and we would join in:

My road is rough and rocky
My cross is heavy to bear
My friends talk about me, I can't find peace anywhere.
I'm tired, labored, sick and sad.
My heart's heavy laden and I'm feeling bad
I know one day I'm going away
I'm going up to heaven to stay.
(Author unknown.)

Then sometimes we would sing *In the Garden* by C. Austin Miles.

I come to the garden alone,
While the dew is still on the roses,
And the voice I hear, falling on my ear,
The Son of God discloses.

My sisters Rose and Willie Mae were members of the school glee club. They taught the family to sing *If I Had a Hammer* by Lee Hays and Pete Seeger. I didn't know at the time that it was a protest folk song written in support of the Progressive Movement. This song has an upbeat tempo that promotes work, activity and love:

If I had a hammer, I'd hammer in the morning,
I'd hammer in the evening, all over this land.
I'd hammer out danger, I'd hammer out a warning,
I'd hammer out love between my brothers and my sisters,
All over this land.

During the long days in the field, we also sang Negro spirituals like *Steal Away to Jesus*. Singing really was an energizing way to get into a rhythm. It was a good time for us. Music lifted our spirits. We made the most of it. Sometimes there were other workers out there, too, and they would join in or say, "Y'all sho can sing."

Songs from Sam Cooke or other popular artists also made the field song list. We mixed it up. We kept it moving.

My sister Willie Mae had a rich alto voice and played the piano. Rose could sing soprano, tenor or alto. Rose could harmonize with anyone on almost any song. Willie and Rose allowed me to sing with them in church as a trio even though I had no singing talent. They would adjust their voices to cover my flaws. Willie and Rose sounded better by themselves, but they allowed me to sing with them because I was their little sister. They carried me.

Both of my parents were very hard workers. They never asked us to do anything they didn't do. If my Dad wasn't with us when we were chopping cotton or picking cotton, he was working elsewhere, planting crops, driving the tractor or tending to cattle and hogs he raised.

Looking back, I know all my work gardening, chopping, picking cotton and cleaning homes helped me develop a strong work ethic, which played a significant part in who I am. Once I reached the point at age nine of saying I don't want to be poor, the seed was planted. Hard work felt normal to me. Long hours of work never caused me to recoil.

As I became a young adult, I started reading about capitalism, how the economy worked, and how some people manage to overcome poverty. I read that if you work one job and live off that job and work a part-time job and invest and save everything you get from the part-time job, you are likely to get ahead quicker. So, I internalized that idea. I knew that no matter how hard I had to work, a job and a-half would still be a lot easier than chopping cotton. I was willing to work. I had nothing to lose. So, I decided to go for it. And I did, eventually working in real estate as my second job. It would prove to be my path to success and financial independence.

Of course, it wasn't easy, and a lot happened along the way. Major life complications I confronted in my early years – and continued to deal with for many years to come – included poor self-esteem, insufficient early education, racism and poverty.

EDITOR'S NOTE: *For readers only interested in Jannie's business story – how she became financially independent working in real estate – please turn to Part II. Her story includes lessons and business practices that will be helpful to others, whether they are beginning or already experienced in real estate sales or investing in real estate.*

Chapter 2

Family Life

Amazingly, my mother, Luella Hudson Carter, picked over 200 pounds of cotton on October 20, 1950, prior to giving birth to me around 9:30 p.m. In a sense, I was born working. All ten of us (my siblings and I) were born in our home on the farm in Halls (Lauderdale County), Tennessee. Dr. C.D. Coleman was the black doctor who provided medical care and delivered babies in their homes. He provided most of the primary health care to black families in west Tennessee.

Mom and my father, William Beasley Carter, named me Jannie Olevia. I'm named Jannie for my father's mother, but her "Jannie" was spelled with one 'n'. My parents intended for the doctor to put Janie on my birth certificate. He made a mistake. My parents had six girls – Lucille, Geraldine, Alline, Willie Mae, Rose and I'm number six. After I was born, my parents had four boys – William Junior, Dennis Charles, Cleo, and Kenneth Bernard. Mom named her three oldest daughters after local teach-

31

ers. All three of them became teachers. She named Dennis Charles and Cleo after doctors. All four of my brothers became doctors. Mom wanted her girls to be teachers and her sons to be doctors.

When I became old enough to ask what happened to my namesake, Mama Janie, Mom said Mama Janie had a nervous breakdown and spent some time in the mental health hospital in Bolivar, Tennessee. Mom said Mama Janie returned home eventually, but she did not seem happy anymore. Mama Janie died of pneumonia on February 12, 1942. She was fifty-eight years old. I wondered what drove Mama Janie to a nervous breakdown. Dad didn't talk much about his mother. Her absence seemed to bring him sadness. Dad talked more about his father.

My Dad

Dad was a farmer. He loved the land and he was a hard worker. He displayed a pleasant personality most of the time. Women around town described my father and his only brother, Anderson Carter, Jr., as handsome. I overheard women talking and giggling about how cute they were. I felt safe growing up on the family farm with my uncle, Aunt Edna (his wife) and their six kids next door.

Neither my Dad nor uncle was tall. They stood about five-foot-eight with a muscular build.

Each had high cheekbones, a prominent forehead, and an olive complexion. Their hair was black and thick with some natural curl. My Dad's eyes were light brown.

Sixth grade is the highest anyone has mentioned my father attaining. He and his two siblings went to the one-room Currin School on an adjoining farm. My Dad and uncle had to work hard to help my grandfather hold on to the farm. Even as young children they worked more than they studied. Yet somehow, Dad and my uncle and aunt could read, write and do arithmetic.

Dad was usually easy-going. However, he did believe in corporal punishment if children didn't obey. That was the thinking back then. That's the model he grew up under and that's what he believed to be in the child's best interest. Dad was a deacon in the church and he would quote scripture about "spare the rod and spoil the child" and that kind of thinking. My mother, though, was the disciplinarian in the family. My Dad worked from sun-up to sundown, and if there was some work that needed to be done after dark, he did it. My mother ran the household.

Mom administered most of the spankings. She used a little switch. She would send you to the willow tree to get your own switch. That was part of your punishment. Her switchings weren't that bad. We didn't really dread my mother's switchings very much. But I got plenty, from the time I was very young until I was about twelve. For example, if we were playing outside and my mother said, when I call you at dark, I want you to be on the front porch or be inside. If you weren't, she would do a switching. So, the next day you would tend to remember, okay it's getting dark, I better get inside. Anything that she told us to do, and we didn't do, she would either threaten us with the switch, or switch us. Spankings became beatings when my dad provided discipline. Fighting each other was a no-no. You just didn't do it. Fighting each other netted us a serious discipline. We learned to hide our fights with each other. If we fought when our parents were not home, none of us would tell them. My parents commanded us to love each other. Immediately after our discipline, our parents would say "Y'all hug and make up."

Dad was a storyteller. He told us ghost stories and he also recalled for us his experience working as a laborer in East Tennessee to earn money during the winter months. He said he was one of the strongest men working in the log camp. We felt proud each time he told this story. He also told us stories Papa had told him and his siblings.

When Papa sneaked away from King William County, Virginia at the age of eighteen, he said he hid on a boat docked on the James River. He heard that Quakers were kind to black people; therefore, when he disembarked the boat down-river, he walked to a Quaker community in Pennsylvania. Papa worked there as a laborer. He said he was treated well. One night a white stranger visited the farmer who had hired Papa. Even though Papa usually ate the evening meal with the farmer and his family, he did not join them for dinner that evening. The next day the farmer asked Papa why. He explained that the white visitor probably did not want to eat with a black man. The Quaker farmer told Papa that he was to eat with them each evening – even if the President of the United States showed up for dinner.

Papa left the Quaker community because he wanted to marry. Even though the farmer told Papa there were many women in the valley he could marry, Papa said they were all white. He was fearful of racial hatred if he married a white woman. So, he moved on to Kentucky where he worked the tobacco fields. From Kentucky he moved to Tennessee. Papa worked loading and unloading boats on the Mississippi River.

One Saturday night a beautiful black woman talked to him at a café. She told him that if he would go with her, she had a small farm they could work and get married and live well together. He followed her to the boat. There was a boat captain and others there. They sailed over to Shoaf's Island. Once there, a white man met him and told him he would be working for him. Papa was hurt to know that the black woman was really working for the white man and tricking black men into coming to this island – an extension of slavery.

After a few weeks, Papa told the white man he wanted to be paid so he could move on. The white owner put a long gun in Papa's face. He yelled, "Red nigger, do you still want to be paid?" Papa's only choice was to say no. He was never paid for his labor. Papa kept working, but he and another man started to plan their escape. One night during Christmas when the owner left the island, Papa and his co-worker tied some logs together and paddled across the cold Mississippi River to Memphis.

We all listened eagerly when dad told us stories – even though we heard these same stories many times during our childhood.

After many years of working and saving, Papa was able in 1904 to buy a 150-acre farm in Lauderdale County Tennessee. He had one old mule and a plow. He struggled to get by.

During the Great Depression, Papa almost lost the farm. He heard that the Federal Bank in Louisville would allow poor farmers to borrow money to hold on to their farms. Papa walked and begged rides during the long journey, almost 300 miles from Halls, Tennessee to Louisville, Kentucky. Papa told his children that it was a lonesome journey and that he was often cold and hungry. After days of walking and hitchhiking, he made it. Papa got the loan and saved the farm. During times in my life when I felt tired and wanted to give up, I thought about Papa walking alone tired and hungry. Somehow, that vision, that story provided the impetus for me to get up and do what I needed to do – whether it was study an extra hour to prepare for an exam or work from 7 a.m. until 10:30 or 11 at night. If Papa accomplished his goal, so could I.

The Farmhouse

The house where I was born was very old and drafty. I have included a picture of it. This house represents the world of poverty into which I was born. It was small and without indoor plumbing. When I was three, Mom and Dad tore down that house and built a 1950's-style house. I guess you would call it a farmhouse. It was white and had a black roof and a little porch. We moved into this home in 1953. It is the only home I remember. It had one indoor bathroom, two bedrooms, a living room, dining room and kitchen.

There were six girls born first. William Jr. was born in 1953. Mom and Dad put all us girls into one bedroom. I remember three of us would sleep with our heads toward the top of the bed, like people normally sleep, and the other three would sleep with our heads at the foot of the bed with our legs going the other way. If somebody kicked somebody at night, they would go and sleep on the little sofa, or on the floor. Six in a bed doesn't sound conducive to a good night's sleep but I slept amazingly well. Perhaps I slept well because I was a child using a lot of energy running and playing all day. More importantly, I thought six sisters sleeping in one bed was normal – that all families slept that way. It was fun at four, five and six years old. I felt safe and I was never lonely.

Some years later, following the birth of my second oldest brother in 1955, my parents added two bedrooms and a second bathroom in 1956. My youngest brother was born in 1961. I will always love the little house on the farm with my nine siblings and two parents. Whenever I see or hear the word 'home', the little farmhouse comes to mind. I lived there from 1953 until I left for college in 1968.

My parents always emphasized the importance of family. One of Dad's stories made that point. It was a story about ten sticks. We did not know when we were young that he was telling his version of Aesop's Fable of the Bundle of Sticks. He told us this story many times. Dad's version follows:

An elderly man had ten sons. He had always taught his sons to respect and love each other. He asked them to work together to defend and support each other, to maintain unity. He reminded his sons that they were more like each other than they were similar to any other living being. During the father's years of strength, he had been able to ensure one brother's cooperation with the other. Now, the father was elderly, weakening, and approaching the end point of his natural life. The father sensed some friction amongst his sons. He called all ten of his sons to his bedside. He told each son to go out and find the strongest stick he could find and return with one strong stick. The sons mumbled at the old man's request, as children often do, but they went out to find a strong stick.

When all ten sons had returned with a stick, the father asked them to gather around his bed. He asked the eldest son to gather the sticks and tie them together in a bundle. He then told the eldest son to try to break the bundle of sticks. The oldest son, who prided himself on his physical strength and on pleasing his father, tried very hard. He used all his strength, but he could not break the bundle of sticks. The father then asked sons number two, three, four and on down the line to try to break the sticks. None of them could break the bundle of sticks. The father then asked the eldest son to untie the bundle and give each son a stick. He told them to break their one stick. They quickly popped the sticks into two parts. The father then said to his sons, "See how easy it is to break one stick. Remember that the bundle could not be broken. The lesson for you, my sons, is clear. Remain together – together you lend strength to each other, apart you can be easily broken. Don't part ways." The sons all hugged each other and promised their father that they would remain together. Their father died peacefully a few days later.

My Dad said, "Where there is unity, there is strength." He asked us to stay together and to always remember this story.

During the 30-plus years I worked in public health, I saw numerous studies and heard presentations about what creates positive health outcomes – what helps people heal quickly, what helps people stay healthy and grow old happily. One thing that often popped up was emotional support, a support group. It could be a church group, a fraternity, a sorority, a family, or close neighbors. The parable of the sticks illustrates that we do better together.

Dad did not tell many stories about his mother. Any mention of her made him sad. He did say that Mama Janie was kind and generous. I am thankful for the stories he told us.

My Mom

In a May 8, 2022, article published on Mother's Day in The Tennessean newspaper, writer Brad Schmitt noted from interviews with my siblings and me that our Mom wanted to go to high school, but there was no high school in Halls for black children at that time. Her parents, who were sharecroppers, could not afford to transport or board her in Ripley, Tennessee. Mom's education stopped at eighth grade. Schmitt wrote: "Carter, bitterly disappointed, swore she'd do better by her kids. She pledged to herself – and later to her 10 kids – that each one of her children would go to college."

Mom was the parent most concerned about our studies and she made sure we did our homework. She was the drum major for education. Dad not so much. I think he would have been all right if all of us had grown up and stayed on the farm. Farming was his love, and he thought a larger farm was the way to advance. He always talked about buying more land. That was my father's vision. My mother's vision, however, was ten college-educated children who had overcome poverty. "Education offers you the best chance for a good life," Mom would say.

Mom was a fantastic woman. Now that I look back, I'm just amazed. She was a manager, a strategist, an advocate for us. She kept a lot of things go-

ing. All our meals were prepared at home. We didn't
have any money to eat out. It wasn't like, okay, I
can take the kids to McDonald's, it's Friday. No, we
could not do that. There was no McDonald's and we
had no money. My mother cooked every meal when
we were growing up. She was a good cook.

Luella Hudson Carter talked very fast and
could get a lot of things out in a minute. Her Dad
had taught her some basic math and some reading.
She completed eighth grade at the one room Mount
Zion Church School in the Double Bridges community of Halls where she grew up. So, my mother really knew more than some of our teachers, sad to
say. But it's true. Back then, black teachers didn't
need a college education to teach. They could teach
right out of high school in rural communities because there were very few blacks with a college
education. If there was one black college educated
person around, they'd make that one the principal
and then make them responsible for the others who
didn't know anything about teaching and learning.
So, my mother was definitely our first teacher. Mom
helped us with schoolwork as much as possible.

Appearance-wise, my mother was a beautiful
brown attractive lady. Both our parents were neat
and clean people. They taught us that cleanliness
was next to Godliness. Mom's hair was straight.
She never used a hot comb, a perm, or anything

that most of us African American women used back in that day. She could just wash her hair, pull it back, and it would look great. She was probably five-foot-three or five-foot-four in height, medium build. Neither one of my parents was ever obese. When she got to be sixtyish and slowed down some, she probably got up to a size fourteen. During our childhood years, Mom was average height, average build, very active, very healthy. She was always moving – a true force of energy.

My mother cooked mostly what we had from our garden and farm. Sweet potatoes, white potatoes, squash, cabbage, corn, green beans, greens, beets, peas, okra, lima beans, and anything else we could grow. I remember digging white potatoes out of the ground just like we did sweet potatoes.

For meat, we mostly had country ham, sausage and chicken. I remember my mother and older sisters ringing the necks of chickens so we could have fried chicken for dinner. I was never assigned the task of killing the chicken though I witnessed the deed many times. The routine killing proceeded as follows: A chicken roaming free in our yard was chased and caught, a broom or mop handle was in hand, the chicken's neck was placed securely under the broom stick with the person's foot on the stick, the person snatched the body of the chicken upward quickly and the neck separated from the body of the chicken. The body was tossed into the yard. The headless chicken flopped around wildly as the life left its bloody body. The chicken was then placed in boiling water, feathers were pulled off, the chicken was cut into pieces, seasoned, breaded with flour and fried to a crispy brown.

We raised and ate a lot of vegetables. My parents fed us less meat because we only had a limited amount of it. Much like today, meat was more expensive than cereals and vegetables. I did not realize until many years later that we ate a mostly healthy diet by default – we had more vegetables and grains than meat.

My mother made delicious chocolate pies, chess pies and coconut pies if she could get a little coconut from the store. The fresh butter from cows on the farm gave our food some real flavor. We never went hungry. I don't know how my parents did it. Mom always cooked. I never heard her say she was tired of cooking. She made lots of good cornbread and homemade biscuits. Sometimes for our morning meal, we would have rice with butter and sugar in it before we went to school. We would have oatmeal some mornings. We didn't have ham and biscuits every day. We had cereal and a plentiful supply of eggs. I remember going to the hen house and shooing a chicken off its nest to get the eggs so Mom could make a chocolate pie for dinner and scrambled eggs for our breakfast the next morning. Sometimes we ate scrambled eggs with homemade biscuits and Mom's homemade strawberry preserves for breakfast. We grew the strawberries.

Mom made delicious biscuits from scratch. She sifted a large mound of flour on to the rectangular wooden board, then reached over with one hand and picked up a handful of shortening (lard) and put it in the center of the flour. Then she blended it by squeezing the flour and shortening through the fingers of her right hand. When the shortening and flour were mixed to her satisfaction, she used her knuckle to create a valley in the center of the mixture. She poured milk into the depressed area and used both hands to blend it into dough which she rolled out and cut into biscuits. She used a cup to cut the biscuits. Then she placed the dozens of biscuits on the greased baking sheet and put them in the already preheated oven. Wa La! About 20 minutes later we had the best homemade biscuits a child could want. As I watched, I wondered how she knew how much flour to start with, how much shortening to add, how long to mix and how much milk to pour. She never measured any ingredients. My Mom worked magic for every meal. I wish I had learned biscuit-making from her.

My parents grew strawberries to eat and to sell for spring income. During strawberry season, we picked strawberries after school and on Saturdays. The taste of West Tennessee strawberries and tomatoes is special, deep and flavorful – a testament to the quality of the soil coupled with the careful care of dirt farmers like my father. Mom would wash a big bowl of strawberries, put sugar on top and mash the berries – juice would ooze into the bowl. We would stir until all sugar dissolved. Then we would spoon the berries onto our plates and sop Mama's homemade biscuits and berries. No spoons or forks for the berries and biscuits. We sopped. It was natural and delicious!

My mother also canned vegetables. I remember washing lots of Mason jars. We grew a lot of green beans, tomatoes and beets. Before we had a deep freezer, she canned huge amounts of vegetables. In the winter, she would make delicious beef soup with those canned vegetables and a small piece of beef.

We didn't have a cellar, but up in the rafters of the hen house there was an area where Dad could store things. There also was a smokehouse. Pork was smoked and cured in the smokehouse. Dad walled off a part of the smokehouse to set potatoes or other items during the winter. I also remember a part of our enclosed back porch where some food was kept for winter.

During Revival Weeks, each woman in the

church prepared a box of food for dinner on the church grounds. The meal was served after the afternoon service and prior to the evening service. It was marvelous food. Each woman prepared what she had in her garden or field. Even though the women didn't seem to discuss who would bring what, the meals would be balanced and fresh and beautiful. Colorful pickled beets, deviled eggs, fried chicken, country ham, corn, okra, butter beans, peas, potato salad, macaroni and cheese, turnip greens, mustard greens, collard greens, yams, pies, cakes, and breads appeared out of those cardboard boxes the ladies carried. Revival food was always delicious and there was always enough. This was an example of community at its best.

My sisters and I were Mom's kitchen assistants. We peeled, chopped, and did what we were told. We didn't do too well on biscuits and pies. My mother didn't like anything wasted, so she didn't encourage us to practice cooking. We were good assistants, so we learned just by being in the kitchen with her.

My mother was fairly intense, much more so than my father. She was the one who would point out errors. She was our strongest advocate and our most severe critic. She could tell you everything you did wrong. She was quicker to tell you what you did wrong than what you did right. Mom and I clashed a lot when I was a teenager. She didn't understand the psychological damage I endured by hearing all the things I did wrong and hearing of hardly anything I did right. I felt devalued, my self-esteem diminished. Mom was just trying to point us in the right direction, and sometimes that felt harsh and abrupt. But that was my mother's personality. On the positive side, Mom would also sit down and play games with us. She was present. She did not leave us to our own devices.

My parents really wanted a boy when I born as the sixth girl. It felt like – once I became aware, and I don't know at what point that was, maybe it was four years old – my brother was the center of their universe. Everybody oohed and ahhed over him, and he was a cute little fella. I didn't like him because he received all the attention. My parents now had their long-awaited son – their special blessing.   They had been married fourteen years and they had six girls. So, when William Jr. came along three years after I was born, they were ecstatic. Dad verbalized his vision of being able to farm more land with my brother doing one task while he did another. I heard Dad say, "We need boys to carry on the Carter family name." I realized the male child was valued more than the female. Dad had one sister, Ovalie, and she got married and left the farm at age fifteen. So, Dad felt like, "Oh I need boys who are going to stay here." Dad and his brother stayed side-by-side and farmed their entire lives. Dad and Mom were boldly and visibly happy to have a son. I felt put down and of minimal importance to my parents. My sisters became my primary care givers and my best friends.

Mom and Dad were good, decent parents. Unfortunately, this fact escaped me during my childhood. They did the best that they knew.

Religion

Every Sunday our parents took us to Mt. Zion Missionary Baptist Church. The services were long. My siblings and I saw gaps in what people said in church and how they acted when they left church. Of course, we were children, and we would have preferred to be at home playing some of that time.

The pastor of our little country church was Rev. George W. Tyus. He preached each Sunday in the town of Dyersburg. Dyersburg was much larger than Halls; therefore, Tabernacle Baptist Church in Dyersburg was home to a congregation that was larger and better educated than rural Mt. Zion. Tabernacle could afford to pay the pastor more. He preached at Tabernacle every Sunday at 11 a.m. On the first and third Sundays in each month, Rev. Tyus would drive to Mt. Zion and preach around 2 p.m.

For some reason, the adults started Sunday

School around 11 a.m. It ended around 12:30. The time between 12:30 and 2:00 p.m. on preaching Sundays (first and third Sundays) was a boring hungry time. We ate breakfast about 9:30. We didn't return home until 5 p.m. In the winter months it was dark when we got home from church. Those Sundays were long days without food. The seven youngest of us did not feel the services addressed our spiritual needs. William Jr., Dennis and I agreed that when we reached adulthood, we would search for spiritual truths.

My parents had a big book of Bible stories with colorful pictures. The book was bound in a padded black vinyl cover. I enjoyed that book. During early childhood, I enjoyed reading, discussing and reciting Biblical stories. I was fascinated by the story of the prodigal son and of Moses going to Egypt and saying, "Let my people go." My siblings and I knew all those stories very well. I understood the stories I read far better than the Sunday sermons I was forced to sit through.

When I was about ten, Rose and I were selected to be youth delegates from Mt. Zion to the Baptist Congress. Our mother, with great pride, dressed us in our Sunday best. Mom combed our hair, put ribbons on our braids, and told us to wipe off our black patent leather shoes. I wore white socks with lace around the top and my little orange dress that had a drop waist and pleats around the bottom – one of my two Sunday dresses.

The Baptist Congress was a group of affiliated churches that met once or twice a year to decide on which Sunday School books to use, annual themes, mission work and other such matters. There were classes and meetings during the day and preaching and singing at night. The location rotated among the several churches.

Religious Prey

After the opening session, one of the preachers said, "Come walk to my office with me." I knew he was a good man, a preacher, a man of God. Our parents taught us to obey adults – especially religious leaders. So, when he smiled at me and asked me to come to his office, I followed him. His office was in the back of the church at the end of a fairly long hallway. After we entered his office, he pushed the door shut. He looked down at me in a way I did not comprehend. I was an innocent ten-year-old child. I had no idea what that look meant. He touched the ribbon on my hair, and it seemed unnatural, awkward, and scary. I started thinking "What is happening here?" He was a tall, athletic built man wearing a dark suit. He wore his hair oiled and brushed back from his forehead. His eyes were just piercing as if they were digging a hole in me. I was nervous and afraid. The door was closed. He stood between me and the door. I was a little girl. He was a big man. He kept staring at me as if he was thinking about what to do next.

As he was stroking the side of my hair, he said, "God likes pretty little girls like you and God wants me to take you to the store to buy you some candy." He told me to meet him at his new blue Buick which was parked in the spot marked "Pastor" on the other side of the church. He opened the office door. I was relieved to dart away. I was able to breathe. I went to find Rose and I told her what he did and said.

"I don't really know what I'm supposed to do. He's the preacher and our parents told us to obey people in authority," I explained. Rose said, "Oh, no, you can't go with him." She was two-and-a-half years older than I. She said, "You stay right here with me the rest of this week. You don't even look at him. He's disgusting." I realized later that Rose saved me from a likely sexual assault as a ten-year-old child. Of course, I've been thankful for her since. She was my guardian angel. She looked after me. I thank God every day for my caring and wise Rose.

Rose went on to tell me that he had gotten a teenage girl pregnant who attended one of the churches he pastored. The girl's family sent her to live with a relative out of state rather than expose the preacher for what he was. Rose said if we told anyone about him approaching me, they would turn it around and blame me. Therefore, Rose advised me to let this be our secret. "Don't tell anyone, not even our parents," Rose said. "Just be quiet and stay away from him." Honestly, that shook my faith. That shook the way I looked at religion. It was a negative influence on me. Wasn't a pastor a spiritual leader in the community? He had impregnated a teenager and churchgoers protected him. How could a pastor use God to lure children into his car to harm them? How could the church members listen to his sermons?

I did not tell my parents about the attempted molestation until I was grown and married. It was during a time when my parents were urging me to attend church regularly. After hearing my story, Mom and Dad seemed very saddened by what had happened to me when I was ten years old. They had been telling me that I should be more religious. My parents had a way of never giving up on what they thought we ought to know, or what we ought to consider. I respected them for that. I was honest with them. They were sorry about the incident. However, they were not surprised that this preacher was a child molester. My parents knew this preacher was corrupt. Why didn't they tell us? Maybe they assumed he would not try anything at the congress. Why do people protect preachers?

Following the discussion with my parents, they seemed to understand my reticence toward religion and church. They stopped badgering me about church. However, they always wanted me to be a devout Christian, like they were. We always had prayers at meals. That was standard operating procedure. No one ate at my parents' home until they blessed the food. They encouraged us to read our Sunday School lessons. Both of my parents read their Bible, and my mother was in the missionary group. Those women met once a week or every other week to discuss missionary lessons and work. They were sincere and true believers.

Generally, we didn't have a Wednesday church service in the country because people worked until dark, which in the summer was 8:30 or 9 at night. So, they would have to rest to start work early the next morning. We did have revivals, and my parents participated. And if there was an extra service on Sunday, they participated.

Am I Cursed?

I was fairly young when Dad told me a Biblical story about Ham. He told it more than once during our life because my brother Dennis who is five years my junior also remembers Dad telling this story. According to what Dad told us, Noah had built the ark for the flood. Noah was instructed by God to get two of every living creature and put them on the ark. God told Noah he was going to destroy the world with a great flood because the world was too sinful. Noah gathered the animals as God instructed him. Sometime after the flood, Noah got drunk. He took off all his clothes, and Ham, the youngest of Noah's three sons, looked upon his father and mocked him. So, God made Ham black as a punishment to Ham for laughing at his father. My siblings and I distinctly remember the story as my father told it.

I remember thinking "Am I cursed? Will this curse stay with me all my life? What can I do if I really am cursed?"

The Holy Bible, King James Version, does not say that Ham laughed at his father's nakedness or that Ham was black. Genesis Chapter 9 Verse 22 says: *And Ham, the father of Canaan, saw the nakedness of his father, and told his two brethren without.*

Ham's two brothers walked backwards with a garment on their shoulders and covered their father's nakedness as reported in Verse 23.

Verse 24 states that *"And Noah awoke from his wine, and knew what his younger son had done unto him."*

Verse 25 reads as follows: *And he* said, (referring to Noah) *Cursed be Canaan; a servant of servants shall he be unto his brethren.* The Bible does not say that Noah or God made Ham black.

This story explains why our father did not want us to marry dark-skinned people. He felt they were more cursed than we were. He literally believed this untruth. None of my siblings know who taught my father this self-denigrating story. Dad passed this on to us, but none of us believed it. Mom remained quiet on this topic. She did not want to undercut my father's teachings.

Talking of such a curse was detrimental to me – a black child. Such stories do not build self-esteem. We were not allowed to debate matters with our parents when we were children. However, after we became adults, we debated this and many other issues with our parents.

Though we could not debate our parents, we held lively discussions among ourselves. Discussion questions included the following: Why did a just God allow Noah to issue such a curse? Noah was the person who was drunk; was Noah punished for his drunkenness? Since Ham was the youngest of Noah's three sons, perhaps he didn't know how to handle his father's nakedness. Instead of cursing Ham, why didn't Noah teach Ham? Noah was not punished for his drunkenness, yet he showed no mercy towards Ham, his son. Was this passage included in the Bible to justify slavery and the mistreatment of some groups of people? Sadly, the idea of a curse troubled me as a young child.

Fourth Grade Horror

I also felt cursed because adults were sometimes mean to me. When I was in fourth grade, I wrote a note during class and passed it to the girl sitting next to me. The teacher saw me and immediately confiscated the note from my friend. Since early childhood I have wanted to be a writer – to say something – hoping I might then be heard. The teacher snatched my note and read it aloud to the whole class. "Boys are different. They are like no one," Mrs. Eddie Lee Williams blurted out. The kids giggled. I started to explain to the teacher what I meant. She told me to shut up.

In fourth grade I didn't like boys. I wanted to explain to her that I meant boys were rude and loud and silly. But she yelled at me to "Shut up! Shut up!" She jerked me by the arm and pulled me to the front of the class. There was a stage in the front of the room where she told me to stand so she could reach my backside without bending over. She seemed angry. She judged me from those eight words. I started to cry. She never allowed me to explain what I meant by those eight words. I was confused.

She walked over to her desk and picked up

the thick wooden paddle. She had never had cause to paddle me before, so I didn't know what to expect. My bladder was full because it was afternoon and I tried to avoid going to the stinking outdoor toilet. Mrs. Eddie Lee Williams pulled the paddle back and hit my bottom as hard as she could. It pushed me forward. The force of the paddle almost knocked me down. The jolt caused my bladder to release its cargo. I wanted to die. Children were laughing. I felt the warm liquid running down my leg into my socks and shoes. I trembled as the puddle enlarged around my feet. She hit me several more times. One boy on the front row yelled out "She whipped the pee out of her."

The teacher angrily told me to go ask the principal to call Mom to pick me up. Mrs. Williams was a member of a very conservative religious group. She wore her dresses very long, almost to her ankles. She misjudged me. Adults during that time said children should be seen but not heard. I was certainly not heard that day.

Mrs. Geraldine Eisom was the principal of Lillian Fountain Grammar School. She looked displeased when I told her I wet my clothes and asked her to call my Mom. She handed me some rough brown paper towels as she looked at me with a hint of pity. Mrs. Eisom spoke to me with a kind calm voice. I was grateful for the brown paper towels she gave me. I wiped my legs, socks and shoes while Mrs. Eisom called my Mom. She said my Mom would be there soon. I told Mrs. Eisom I would go to the restroom and then wait for Mom on the front steps of the school. Mrs. Eisom's classroom adjoined my fourth-grade classroom. I am sure she witnessed my beating.

I ended up at that stinking outhouse after all. It was a place to hide from my laughing classmates who witnessed the humiliating fact that I urinated on myself. As I stood in that stinking open sewerage house, I wondered why the teacher wanted to beat me. Why did my eight little words make her angry? I was not guilty of any sin. Why didn't she allow me to explain what the eight words meant? I cried some more, then walked beside the school to the front steps and folded my head in my lap. I did not dare go back to the classroom to get my books. I went home that day with empty hands and a broken spirit.

When Mom drove up in front of the school, I ran to her car. As I sobbed and told her what happened, she seemed sad. Mom assured me it would never happen again. Mom never hit us with solid heavy objects. Mom disciplined us with willow tree switches. The next morning Mom drove me to school. She met with the principal and fourth grade teacher. None of the teachers ever hit me again.

The idea that I might have been cursed found fertile ground in my childhood mind. From my immature view of the world, I saw proof that I was cursed – shabby school, partially destroyed textbooks, inadequately trained teachers, the need to miss school some days to work on the farm, the crushing reality that my brothers enjoyed my parents' devoted attention and the message from Dad that Ham was cursed and made black. I saw and felt what being black meant in my community. Benefits that whites enjoyed were denied to blacks. White schools were well-staffed and equipped to prepare white kids for college. When I walked into the clothing store, I saw a water fountain marked White and one marked Colored. When we went to the Dairy Queen, Dad would get us an ice cream cone. Small cones were a nickel in the late 1950s. So, in the harvest season when Dad was selling cotton, he could afford a nickel cone for all of us. We had to pull around to the back of the Dairy Queen and they would pass the cones through the window. The white people could go in, sit down and eat, or go to the front window. Blacks were expected to live in the shadows and get by. This seemed unfair, unjust. Cursed?

The Farm

The farm was one place where I didn't feel cursed. It provided open space to breath and a place to work, play and separate from conflict.

When Papa died, the land was divided among his three children. Dad inherited about 50 acres and he and Mom purchased another 20 acres or so after they were married. They worked about 70 acres. Most of that was for cotton and soybeans. Dad also grew what he called truck patches: tomatoes, greens, purple hull peas, corn and strawberries. He also raised hay for the cattle. Those were the primary crops.

My Dad and his brother, Anderson, lived side-by-side on the small farm that Papa Carter had owned. Uncle Anderson purchased additional acres, rented his sister Ovalie's 50 acres, and rented and worked other farms. Dad and Uncle Anderson each raised cattle and hogs. My Dad raised 12 to 14 cows each year. He maintained a couple of cows for milk and the others were raised and sold for income.

Once a year, they would have hog-killing day. My uncle also had a couple of horses. We had chickens and a hen house when I was very young, and that's where we got our eggs. Dad milked the cows. My mother and my older sisters churned the butter into cute little pounds. Mom would sell the butter to women who lived in town or to the women whose husbands did not raise cows. They were what we called city people. They liked the fresh farm butter. The sale of butter provided cash that our family desperately needed.

Sometimes Dad and my uncle would kill a cow and we would have beef to eat. Dad had more hogs than cattle because the hogs didn't require much land. They didn't need to graze like cattle. Dad just put a bunch of hogs in the pen and threw corn, table scraps and whatever in the feeding trough and hogs would be fine. Hogs ate everything; cows did not. We ate more pork than beef.

Our farm was small, but it provided a stable life for us. We took some pride in the fact that Papa Carter, who had been born a slave, somehow found a way to leave us a foundation.

Chapter 3

Traumatic Transitions

When I started school in 1957, there was no kindergarten. I went to Lillian Fountain Grammar School in Gates, Tennessee, in Lauderdale County. The school had four classrooms and a little kitchen. Four rooms for grades one through eight. There were two grades in each room. One teacher taught both grades. As you can imagine, we weren't learning very much. During the 1950s, black students who completed high school were allowed to teach school. As a result, many of our teachers were not prepared to teach. We were severely hampered in early childhood learning.

Sometimes if there was an advanced child who was smart or their parents helped them learn something specific, he or she would help teach. If there was a child in the class who understood math, for example, the teacher would tell the child, "Go help Cora Lee learn how to do subtraction." My brother Cleo still talks about how well he taught first grade when he was a second-grader.

My maternal grandfather, Louis Hudson, had finished high school and his father's dream was for his son to go to college. Daddy Louis refused to go. For him to finish high school was a great big deal back then. He didn't send his children to high school because the high school for black kids was about 10 miles away in the town of Ripley, Tennessee. Ripley was the county seat and there was no transportation for black kids to get from their homes to the county high school. My mother's dream had been to go to high school, but Daddy Louis would not send her. When she was sixty-nine, she finally got her General Education Development certificate (GED). My mother was a happy sixty-nine-year-old high school graduate. She realized part of her dream at that point.

My mother was passionate about education. Our maternal grandfather, to his credit, did teach his children some basics, some things he had learned in high school. So, my mother was able to help us. In fact, she was a better teacher than most teachers who provided instruction to me in elementary school. My mother deeply valued education. She would always tell us that education offered our best chance of escaping poverty. Mom felt that having a farming income that was dependent on the weather was risky. My father touted the virtues of farming – working for himself, watching things grow, living and working on his own land. Mom talked to us about going to college.

The elementary school I attended from grade one through eight looked like a house, and since that time, it has been sold, remodeled and is now being used as a duplex. One thing that I remember was that we didn't have indoor plumbing at the school. I dreaded going to school because of the outside toilet. The smell was nauseating. Sometimes kids were sick, they vomited on the floor. I tried not to go to the restroom at school. Sometimes there was no toilet paper. Paper was scarce. Of course, there was no running water, just this stinking wooden outhouse out back of the school. It was perched on the hilly side of the back schoolyard. It looked like a small wooden closet from the outside. Inside there were two wooden stools sitting over open holes dug fairly deep into the ground. We sat on the wooden stools and eliminated into the deep stinking open hole. We could look down into the hole and see the horrible collection of human waste; the odor was almost unbearable on warm days. When it was cold, I shivered when I pulled my clothes down to use the wooden outdoor toilet. Thankfully in 1953, our parents had built our two-bedroom, one-bath home. One bath for a large family today may sound like a burden, but in my world in 1957 it was a luxury not available at our black elementary school.

At school, I enjoyed reading and discussing stories. Geography was interesting to me. I was fascinated to hear that the world was big – much bigger than West Tennessee. Perhaps I could escape to a place where I did not have to chop cotton. I also liked storytelling. When I was in fourth grade, I entered a storytelling contest in the county, and I won third place. I received a certificate. I remember the story started off, "In days of yore, there lived a Queen. She was old and ugly. But her daughter, who of course was a princess, was young and beautiful." I didn't write it. I memorized and recited the short story. We weren't allowed to read the story. Back then, people were expected to memorize things. My mother could recite a poem with sixteen stanzas. She wouldn't miss a word. Our father could recite long poems and scriptures. One poem my father recited to us was "When You Educate a Negro, You Unfit Him to Be a Slave." Parents and teachers expected children to memorize long passages. My parents purchased a cute little green dress and black patent shoes for me to wear to the storytelling contest. That was one time when I felt that maybe they liked me as much as they liked my brothers.

Math was a challenge for me. We weren't taught much math at school, but Mom did teach us enough arithmetic to become functional.

I didn't really pay very much attention to

school. I was playful and I didn't focus. I was an okay student just because my mother wouldn't accept anything less. I couldn't go home with F's and D's and teachers' notes saying that I disrupted class or sassed a teacher. If we disrespected a teacher, the penalty was certain and severe. None of us ever disrespected our teachers. Mom made clear her expectations of us. At the end of the school day, we had a home-cooked meal. When we got off the school bus at the end of our little dirt/gravel road, we savored the smell of the white beans or meatloaf or whatever Mom was cooking. She cooked for us every day.

During early childhood, I was not passionate about school, but I couldn't stay home either. If I tried to fake an illness, Mom would feel my forehead. She could tell whether I had a fever. If my forehead was not hot, I went to school and that was it. Mom did not own a thermometer when we were growing up. Her hand was her thermometer. Our mother was our counselor, teacher, pediatrician, and everything else. Mom was not easily fooled.

Sometimes Dad required us to stay home and help on the farm. Our schoolwork fell behind. Mom tried to help us study at night and keep up with the class. After two days of missing school, Mom would urge Dad to let us go back to school. I distinctly remember one time Dad told us he needed us to skip school and pick cotton three consecutive days. Mom came to our bedroom after we had picked hard the second day. She told us to get up the next day (day three) and dress for school. She said she would take the blame. When Dad saw us dressed for school – he was upset. He said we could lose the farm. He vented his frustrations and fears, and he mentioned compounding interest. We all kept quiet and ran to the bus when it arrived. In the fall in West Tennessee, all black schools had an early autumn break of about six weeks to pick cotton. It was usually during late September and all of October. We were the cotton pickers – a large part of the agricultural labor force. Mechanical cotton pickers were not available or widely used during this time in history (1950s and early 1960s).

Our elementary school schedule included lots of free play time called recess. At recess we played games like hopscotch, jumping rope, baseball, tag or whatever we could come up with to amuse ourselves. In addition to recess, we spent copious amounts of the school day helping Mama Lacy prepare and serve lunches or washing dishes after lunch. We spent chunks of time in non-classroom non-learning activities.

I got along well with most of the kids in my school. Once in a while, someone would talk ugly to us and say something like, "Y'all think y'all white. I'll kick your yellow ass." Kids can be horrible to other kids. But fortunately, I attended school alongside my sister, brothers, and my uncle's three kids. We all looked alike and our last name was Carter. There were enough of us in the same age group to defend each other. After a few skirmishes, the other kids realized they could not bully us. We survived pretty well. Basically, we had some pleasant friendships in elementary school. Some schoolmates perceived us as belonging to another group, but we weren't another group. What we wanted was what, I believe, most people want – to belong – to be a part of a community, to live in peace.

One particular bullying incident still lingers in my elementary school memory. When I was in seventh grade, Millard Yancy grabbed me on my behind. I slapped him hard across his face. He ran away. As I was boarding the school bus at the end of that day, he ran up behind me and hit me with his fist in the back of my head. The blow to my head was extremely hard. I saw stars as I struggled dizzily onto the bus and dropped down on the first seat. My cousin got on the bus and noticed me rubbing the back of my head. I told him what Millard had done during the day and how he slammed me with his fist as I was boarding the bus. Millard had grinned as he walked away towards his home. My cousin, Anderson Carter III, who was muscular, older and in eighth grade, told me not to worry.

He said he would take care of things the next day. I don't know what my cousin did or said to Millard the next day, but Millard never bothered me again.

My mother made sure we were dressed well for school. She didn't have money, but she had a lot of pride. We were always clean. I think we looked pretty nice. Everything is relative to its environment. If I had been in Manhattan or some other upscale community, I'm sure we would have felt really poor and disadvantaged. But almost all of the kids who went to school with us were sons and daughters of sharecroppers. Other than the teachers, we were probably dressed better than others at school. Perhaps this is one reason they would pick on us from time to time. They said we thought we were this or that. We didn't think we were anything special. We were just poor kids, but our mother made sure we made a good impression.

Our parents urged us to be neat and clean. They were excellent managers. I remember getting on the bus one day and at the very next stop, our cousins got on the bus. One of the younger girls had urinated on herself during the night and her leg was ashy. You could see where the urine had run down her leg and dried on her brown skin. I thought, why didn't her mother tell her to wash herself? Our mother was clean and organized. We had very little cash, but Mom looked at us before we left home.

She surveyed us. Mom was attentive.

Mom knew the women who could sew and sometimes they would make us clothes. Mom would get some cheap fabric and they would make us a dress. She also befriended a white lady who worked at the clothing store. This lady got lots of clothes for her daughter, Kay. When Kay was tired of the clothes, Miss Margaret sold them real cheap to Mom. We liked them. They were usually colorful and well-made. Our black schoolmates didn't know these were Kay's secondhand clothes; they only saw that we were well-dressed. Our parents were very resourceful. They had lived through the Great Depression (1929 – 1941) and they could make something out of nothing. I'm still amazed now when I reflect on those childhood days. My parents worked wonders. They will always be my heroes.

We lived in a rural area several miles from school, so we did not walk to school. Some of my older sisters had been forced to walk to elementary school before there were buses for black kids. They remember being very cold. Finally, my mother learned how to drive so she could take my older sisters to school on cold days. Many women of Mom's generation never learned to drive. By the time I started school, there was a bus for black children. I rode the bus every day.

When I think about elementary school, I remember the differences between the black school and the white school. The white elementary school was about two blocks from ours. It was a nice red brick building with indoor plumbing. I was told that each grade had a separate classroom. I never went inside the white elementary school. The white school had air conditioning and nice playground equipment.

They had new books. We got their leftover books. Sometimes they wrote ugly racial slurs in their books because they knew their used books would be sent to us. Sometimes they'd tear out pages and mark through text. We missed out on whatever information was on those pages. We told our mother and she instructed us to do the following: "You lean over to your classmate and ask to borrow their book. Look at what's on that page. Most of the time, the same page won't be torn out of your book and their book. Make a note of what's missing in your book, say thank you and give their book back. Then you'll know as much as the white kids know." I did this throughout grades 1 through 10 – the entire time I was enrolled in an all-black school. Consequently, when some people argue that everyone has had an equal shot at a good public education, I know it is not the case. It's not the real-life experience for people who grew up in a segregated South.

Mom wanted us to learn. She expected us

to overcome barriers. Years later, I realized that Mom's formula was a positive formula for life: acknowledge the barrier at hand, devise a method to overcome it, move forward.

Neither I nor my classmates ever had an opportunity to interact with any of the white kids during our early years because we went to separate schools and churches. We drank from separate water fountains. If we had a nickel to go to the Dairy Queen, we went to the side or back window. Whites could go inside. So, there was no opportunity to interact. My brothers had a different experience after integration happened. All four of my brothers received an excellent education in the integrated school system. I understand that there are good people who just don't understand there has been an unequal dispensation of justice and resources. It depends on when and where you grew up, and what reality was at that point.

I didn't really think about the separate and unequal schools or focus on it much at the time. When I walked by the white school, which was fairly often because the principal would send us to the little town store, I looked at the white kids playing on the new equipment, and they seemed really happy. I thought, wow, that must be nice. Their school up on the hill was always very pretty, the lot was pretty. So, I had a little jealousy, but my parents didn't allow us to sit around and moan and complain about what others had. Their message to us was, "Be thankful for what you have and make the most of what you have." That was their attitude.

I think Dad was conflicted about the Bible story of Ham and the curse. Dad basically got along with everybody. I think he just accepted the world the way it was. He and my Mom were focused on making a living and taking care of us. They didn't want us to feel sorry for ourselves. I am glad they didn't. Childrearing – I've realized since being a parent – is a very difficult job. So, if they had the attitude of, "Oh we're pitiful and broke and dirt farmers and we don't have the opportunities that other people have," we might have had a whole different outcome. I salute them. If I set aside the story of Ham's curse, their attitude was probably as healthy as possible for us at that time in history. I accept that they did the best they could do.

I distinctly remember the school lunches at our black elementary school. Each day, Mrs. Eisom, the principal, and the cook, Mama Lacy, would decide what we were going to eat. I think the principal had to wait until she collected the 15-cent payments to determine what she could afford to feed us each day. After she collected the lunch money from the students, she would send a couple of us to the store. That's when we would pass the white school. Walking past a place is different than riding past. When walking past, I saw the school from a different angle and for a longer interval. The store was about a mile away. We'd get a head of cabbage for Mama Lacy, the school cook, to make some slaw to go with the beans. A lot of days we had white beans, coleslaw, and cornbread. Mama Lacy also made delicious homemade rolls. She was a good cook. I didn't realize until much later that we were missing prime learning time because the principal would always send two of us to the store, almost every day. She never sent just one. She would send the students she thought were already good students or who wouldn't run off with the change – the ones who would just go to the store and come back. On most days, the principal instructed us to bring her a pint of ice cream. We didn't get to share in the ice cream. That was Mrs. Eisom's treat.

During the late 1950s and early 1960s the United States government distributed food directly to poor people. The food was butter, cheese, peanut butter, rice, powdered milk, and canned pork with gravy. Now, our parents didn't get it, but the schools got some. So, a lot of days we would have pork and gravy. I don't know if the county gave what was left over to the schools, or if they made an allotment to the poor schools. I remember having rice. And, we had macaroni and cheese. Everything

Mama Lacy cooked tasted good. The government butter was pure butter and the cheese was good, too. Sometimes farmers would bring food to the school. I remember Dad would give a bushel of sweet potatoes or something to the school. Other parents would also donate food to the elementary school.

The combination of government food donations, fresh produce given to the school by parents and Mama Lacy's exceptional cooking skills ensured that we had good hot meals for our 15 cents. Mama Lacy prepared these meals on a wood burning stove. I didn't realize when I was walking to that store that I should have been learning some grammar, math and geography. When you're a child and the principal tells you to go to the store, you think that's fun. Most of us students felt it an honor to be selected by the principal to go to the store. Then you come back from the store and enjoyed a super long recess. A lot of my elementary learning time was spent walking back and forth to the store, playing during recess and helping to serve lunch and wash dishes after lunch. If I had not learned some things at home from Mom and my siblings, I would have been illiterate. After grade eight at Lillian Fountain, it was now time to enter high school.

Halls Consolidated High School

In the ninth and tenth grades I attended the all-black Halls Consolidated High School. It was better than elementary in that they didn't send me to the store to get food for lunch. The schoolhouse was better. It was red brick with indoor restrooms! The school wasn't large, but it did have a band room and a small gym with a stage on one side and bleachers on the other so we could have basketball games, plays or the chorus could render a concert on the stage. It was far better than the elementary school.

Halls Consolidated was the black high school for people in Halls, Tennessee, and the rural northern portion of Lauderdale County. Teachers didn't always impart much knowledge , but they held regular classes. During some years, school officials couldn't recruit really good teachers to Halls Consolidated because it was a small town and Lauderdale County was a poor county. Lauderdale County couldn't pay as much as Memphis, Jackson, Nashville or Dyersburg. Seasoned teachers would go where they could get higher pay and enjoy a higher quality of life. Several teachers who taught at Halls Consolidated only taught there until they found a better job elsewhere.

Even at Halls Consolidated, I started to realize that most of the children who had attended the black elementary school in Halls knew more than those of us who had attended Lillian Fountain Grammar in nearby Gates. I thought, oh well. I talked to boys, played, and I did the minimum. I didn't do a whole lot. I learned more than I did in elementary school, but I wasn't where I should have been. I should have buckled down and studied and tried to learn what I could to begin to fill in my elementary school learning gaps. However, I faked being disinterested rather than admitting my deficits. I was a wayward child, an unfocused adolescent. I was mumbling through life at this point. I had a few friends. My main and dearest friend was a girl my age. She was my uncle's stepdaughter. She was smart. Gloria Vanessa Williams wanted to compete with me for grades, but I wasn't interested in competing. When we were freshmen, Gloria said to me "I wish I could go to that white school so I could use their library." If we had competed to see who could earn the highest grades, Gloria would have won handily. Gloria had an adequate elementary education. No way was I going to compete with her. I realized that I was academically behind. I attempted to cover it up by acting silly, pretending to be disinterested in learning, and focusing on boys.

Resources were limited at Halls Consolidated. There were not enough typewriters for typing class. Students took turns trying to learn to type. Lab equipment, materials and chemicals were scarce. It was literally impossible for students at Halls Consolidated to learn what most high school chemistry and biology students were learning.

Richard Nance, Pamela Dunigan, Janice Currin and Earlene Macklin were my other dear classmates and friends at Halls Consolidated and throughout high school. They were all strong students. Richard, like me, had attended Lillian Fountain. He, like me, had older siblings at home from whom he had learned some things. One of our exceptional Halls Consolidated teachers was Mrs. Mary Julia Rhodes, a proud black woman whose parents had been educators. Mrs. Rhodes taught science to all freshmen; she never wasted class time. She was well-dressed and her lectures were organized. She asked us questions and gave pop quizzes. Mrs. Rhodes complimented us when we answered her inquiries correctly. She taught and she was impressive. I still remember the definition of inertia she required us to learn. "A body at rest will remain at rest until acted upon by an equal and opposite force." What a difference a teacher makes!

My sister Rose graduated high school in 1965. That was the last class to graduate from all-black Halls Consolidated. I was the only one in our immediate family in high school in 1965-66. My brothers were all in elementary school.

Halls High School

Integration happened our junior year. There were more than enough typewriters, lab equipment and all other resources for learning. The library was large and well- organized. Gloria got her wish to use the Halls High Library. We were forced to go to the integrated school because officials closed the black high school and made it clear that all students would attend Halls High. It was stressful. One thing that made it super stressful for me was my lack of preparation for high school. I had been playing school for ten years, and then I landed in a real school where every minute of class time was about learning. I remember wondering how I would handle this transition. When we went into the integrated school, they called the roll as soon as the bell stopped ringing. After the roll call, teachers started teaching. No laughing and talking and acting out. They were preparing kids to go to the University of Tennessee, Ole Miss, and the University of Alabama. When kids left Halls High, they were prepared (at least those who wanted to be prepared) and that was the expectation. They would be able to matriculate wherever they wished to go in the world. I was ill-prepared because I didn't do much at Halls Consolidated and I had not been taught much in elementary school. I found myself a junior in high school with an inadequate elementary education. I realized that I needed knowledge. It was time to pay attention.

There was a school counselor at the integrated school who talked to us about what we planned to do in two years after completing high school. "In two years, you'll be an adult," she said. I told her maybe I could be a secretary. The counselor enrolled me in typing and shorthand. They asked all of us, black kids and white kids, what we planned to do in adulthood.

I took typing and shorthand. The lady who taught the business classes, Mrs. Smith, was from Mississippi. She was married to the pharmacist in Halls, who owned and ran Smith Pharmacy. Mrs. Smith was very confident in herself and in her ability to teach. I don't know how or why, but for some reason, she saw something positive in me even though I didn't know very much.

Mrs. Smith's expectation was that after she dictated a letter, we would transcribe and punctuate it correctly. In the world of work, she said we would be expected to take dictation, transcribe it, and hand an error-free document to the boss for signature quickly. That's the way she was, no nonsense. I was a junior. Mrs. Smith told the class that shorthand was only offered to juniors and seniors because she did not teach grammar and punctuation.

"You really should have learned that in elementary school and honed it to perfection in the ninth and tenth grade," she said. As a junior, English was mostly literature, she added. After she realized several of us did not know much, she took the time to teach us nine uses of the comma. She advised us to borrow a ninth-grade grammar book and study on our own.

Mrs. Smith realized what the problems were, and she talked to us about the importance of listening and focusing. She was an excellent teacher, a white, small-statured lady, forceful and clear about what she expected of us. She treated us well. She was a great teacher who made me feel that I needed and wanted knowledge. I realized that I could learn. I had missed years of learning; I really needed to pay attention. She was very direct and honest. She didn't make a lot of small talk. She would say "You're here to learn and this is what I want you to learn today." She was strictly business. She taught the business courses and that was her line of thinking. She was a good lady and a positive influence on my life. I didn't know at the time that my first full time job would be a clerical job – utilizing the shorthand, typing and office skills I learned in Mrs. Smith's classroom in Halls, Tennessee.

When I first went to the integrated school, white students were stand-offish, and understandably so. We didn't know each other. We had never interacted. So, it was new for them, and it was new for us. I felt like they didn't want us there. I believe some white students felt we were invading their space. The way we black kids dealt with it was to stay to ourselves as much as we could. So, if a teacher didn't make us sit every other seat, or something like that, all black kids would sit together, and all whites would sit together. We just hung together. We shared the lunchroom and all school facilities but clearly during this first year of integrated schools, we all felt more comfortable with our own group.

Soon after I started school at Halls High, a white teacher criticized the spelling of my first name. She pointed it out in class when she was calling the roll. The English teacher, Mrs. Steel, said to me "You have two 'n's in your name. It should be pronounced Jan-ney with the two 'n's – not Janie as you pronounce it." I felt this was the teacher's way of letting us black kids know she did not want us in her class. I dropped my head and remained quiet the remainder of the class. Calling me out in class this way made me feel that the English teacher was calling my parents stupid also. One of my classmates told Mrs. Smith what Mrs. Steel said to me. Mrs. Smith asked me whether Mrs. Steel called me out in class in the manner the other student detailed. I said, "Yes ma'am." Mrs. Smith took me by the hand. We marched down to Mrs. Steel's room and Mrs. Smith asked Mrs. Steel to step into the hallway. Mrs. Smith looked Mrs. Steel squarely in the eye and said, "The rule is I can spell my name one way and pronounce it another way. Do not harass this child about her name anymore." Mrs. Steel mumbled an okay and walked away.

I was amazed that a white teacher would defend me from another white teacher. I believe Mrs. Smith wanted us to know that she had our backs – that she was a fair-minded person. It made me feel better about Halls High School. After that incident, I did not feel the need to explain to people about the spelling of my name. My paternal grandmother, whose name was given to me, spelled her name with one 'n'. The doctor who delivered me inadvertently put two 'n's on my birth certificate.

During my eleventh-grade year at Halls High (my first year there), I took Home Economics – Home Ec as they called it. We learned practical skills like cooking and sewing. For example, the teacher taught us how to make a tuna casserole. Basically, the recipe consists of macaroni, cheese, chopped onion, a can of green peas, a can of cream of mushroom soup and a small can of tuna. We prepared the meal in class and ate it within the allotted time. The teacher showed us the food receipt; this meal could be prepared at that time for 25 cents per person for a family of four or $1.00. The meal included brownies and regular saltine crackers. Remember this was 1966. Since that class in 1966, I have prepared and enjoyed this meal with my family many times. Tuna casserole is one of my children's favorite meals.

Halls High offered some extracurricular activities, but I could not participate because I worked for a white family after school and on Saturdays. My family needed the money. James Hansford owned the furniture store in Halls. One Saturday when Mom was in town, his wife Jean approached Mom and said they had several children and they needed help from time to time. She asked Mom if we could help out. Of course, we needed money, so Mom said yes. Rose, who graduated in 1965, worked for them first, and then for a little while, we both worked for the Hansfords. When Rose left in 1965, I became the main worker. We served dinner parties, cleaned the house and babysat. Miss Ella Currin, an elderly black lady, had been Jean's cook and maid for decades. Miss Ella had worked for Jean's parents – and Miss Ella could cook! She was now too old to do the cleaning and babysitting – she just cooked. Miss Ella, Rose and I ate after the Hansfords finished their meal and left the dining room.

They paid us, but Mom took most of the money. We got a little bit of it. She'd give us enough to buy feminine hygiene products and a pair of stockings – something like that. My mom managed the money. When I was a child, people were paid $3 per day for chopping cotton. The Hansfords paid us 50 cents an hour. Therefore, we could earn as much or more with the Hansfords if we worked at least six hours. I remember being on my knees polishing their red tile front porch. The cleaning work was sometimes hard, but chopping cotton was harder. They would sometimes give us a tip at the end of a long day.

Having the job taught me to follow instructions and be ready on time because they picked us up. It also contributed to my work ethic. I was really glad to have the job. I knew it wasn't something that I wanted to do as an adult, but it made me feel useful as a child. My family was strapped for cash. So, Mom used some of the money we earned to buy things our family needed. Plus, it gave us a little spending money. I valued the job.

The Hansford's one-story red brick home sat on an elevated, expertly manicured lot with a huge flower and vegetable garden. When Rose and I mentioned these niceties to Mom, she said "That is the way educated rich people live." Mom advertised education at every possible opportunity.

Part of the time we spent working might have been better spent studying. However, the job itself provided an up-close lesson into how wealthy people lived. My first part-time job influenced the way I live today. One-story brick homes have remained my favorite.

Life-Changing

I tried to settle into high school, but unfortunately boys paid attention to me, and I liked the attention. My parents didn't seem to notice me much. My life derailed. I became pregnant my junior year of high school. Pregnancy was a major issue. I was already behind academically due to a lack of an elementary education. My parents were poor. I had no idea what being a parent meant. I had just gotten into the integrated school, and I was learning. I wondered whether I had doomed myself to poverty forever!

I think part of the reason I got pregnant was that I devalued myself. I'm not putting that on my surroundings because I realize my brain was not working as it should have been working. I learned years later that the adolescent brain is not fully developed. I did not properly link actions to consequences. I did not enjoy sex at that age. I just liked the attention. I had issues like many adolescents do. As a teen, I had issues with my parents. I felt my parents showed preferential treatment to my brothers. This angered me.

Another part of the puzzle of why I became

pregnant was that my father didn't think that we should like really dark men. That bothered me. This really dark guy showed an interest in me. I just wasn't thinking. I wasn't being smart.

It was a very brief relationship, and it was a shock to me to get pregnant. But looking back, I don't know what I expected to happen. Like many teenagers, I guess I felt invincible, like it wouldn't happen to me. It wasn't intentional, but I was reckless. It's similar to kids who go out driving 100 miles an hour on the road and think nothing will happen; this is what happens to other people. That's what makes those teen years so dangerous. It was not what I wanted to happen, but my actions made pregnancy possible.

I was humiliated and embarrassed. I felt really stupid, and I was ashamed. I considered suicide. I wondered whether I had inherited Mama Janie's mental issues as well as her name.

I realize now how fragile those teen years are. Regrettably, some teens just don't make it through. I'm thankful that I did. It's dangerous to be a non-thinking teenager. I think part of me was trying to get back at my Dad and I was devaluing myself, not really understanding and not being able to do analytical thinking and consequential thinking. For example, if I do X, Y might happen. Therefore, this action is not worth the risk – the consequence.

My parents, of course, were in shock when my sister Rose told them I was pregnant. I could not bring myself to say "I am pregnant" to my parents. Instead, each day I became more confrontational with Mom. One day Mom said, "What is wrong with you?" Rose spoke up and said, "Jannie is pregnant." They had reared five girls, and none had become pregnant in high school. It was hard for them, very hard. My Dad asked me three times if I had been raped. I said no. Dad seemed at that time to harbor pent-up anger. He wanted to do something. The last thing I wanted was my Dad in trouble due to my craziness. It was not rape. It was teenage risk-taking, stupidity and immaturity.

My parents were upstanding members in the community. They were big-time church people, and to have a pregnant unmarried teenager was devastating for them. I told them I would give the baby up for adoption. I remember my mother saying, "We don't give away our children." So, I thought, well I'll just kill myself. That'll be the easiest thing. That way, they'll bury me and then they'll stop talking about it and go on with their lives. I was really at a low point. I still don't know for sure why I didn't commit suicide. I thought about different methods. I knew where my Dad's guns were. I rejected the idea; guns seemed too messy and violent. I read somewhere that you could just take a huge amount of aspirin, go to sleep and die. I decided that method was a lot easier than guns. I did not talk to my parents about suicide. I talked with them about giving my child up for adoption because I didn't want to saddle them with added responsibility. My parents never knew I considered suicide.

The baby's biological father was absent. He didn't have any involvement or help me with the baby. He was out of it. He continued his life playing basketball and dating. He went on with his life as if nothing had happened. My Dad was right about his character. The school prom was in May. He invited another classmate and went to the prom. I felt completely messed over and rejected. On prom night I was big and pregnant.

Mrs. Smith had told me at the end of the second grading period that I qualified to get into the Beta Club, which was for serious students, for students who made good grades. I don't remember what my grades were that first semester. I know that I studied. Later in the school year when Mrs. Smith found out I was pregnant, she said to me, "We can't induct you into the Beta Club because Beta Club requires solid character traits as well as academic performance." She said it in a nice way. She wasn't mean. I told her I understood. I was thinking to myself, "Mrs. Smith, Beta Club is the least of my worries. I'm thinking about whether to go on living or throw in the towel." Mrs. Smith was nice in her approach. She seemed sad about the whole matter.

Judgment

One thing that made pregnancy worse for me and my parents was the treatment I received from the church. My mother told me that I must attend a special church meeting. Mom and Dad said that having a baby out of wedlock violated church doctrine. So, they were told that I should appear at the church meeting, and I would be voted out of the church. In other words, I would be de-churched, expelled, exiled. This must have been in March or April because I was visibly pregnant and expecting to give birth in May.

I shall never forget that church meeting. They had a brief devotion, a congregational song, scripture and prayer. Then they started the meeting. The secretary gave a financial report. They all kept looking over at me. I realized that I was their entertainment for the evening – their main event, their entrée. What is it about humans that cause us to enjoy witnessing embarrassing, painful and humiliating episodes of other people?

The preacher asked me to come up front and face the congregation. He asked if I had anything to say. My mother had told me on the way to the church meeting to say I made a mistake and I was sorry. That's what I said. Then the preacher asked the members if they had anything to say. Most of them just stared at me. There was this bench-creaking silence. Then the preacher said, "According to the rules of the church, we have to ask you to separate from the church until after you deliver the baby. After delivery, you can come back and ask forgiveness for your sins." I said, "Yes sir." I could hardly see my parents' faces through my tears. I felt humiliated. My parents were embarrassed. I remember thinking that my parents deserved better from me. I will never forget that night. At the lowest point in my life, the church ostracized me. They cast me out. I was relieved to get back to the church pew and hear the final benediction. They said, "May God watch between me and thee while we are absent one from the other." Wow! I thought, "Will God watch over me while I am absent from the church even though the church members sent me away?"

The ride home was filled with emotional anguish. I wept. My mind raced and skipped. I sensed my parents' pain and embarrassment. I thought about the preacher at another church who had tried to molest me when I was an innocent ten-year-old. That preacher impregnated a teenager. The preacher was never de-churched. Nobody ever called a church meeting. But here I was. A child is easy prey.

My thoughts turned like the wheels on the

car. I don't remember everything I said on that ride home. However, I do remember reminding my parents that a preacher was caught in bed with another man's wife and neither the preacher nor the married woman was expelled from the church. Preachers were supposed to be spiritual leaders. Yet nobody held them accountable. Ridiculing a teenager seemed easy and enjoyable to the church membership.

In the midst of my weeping ride home, I started thinking about cutting my wrist, sitting quietly and ending it all. I seriously considered different methods. Later in life when I started working in public health and I attended a suicide prevention seminar, I realized how close I had come to suicide. The presenter/psychologist described the state of mind I was in after the church meeting. She said when people start thinking about specific methods and evaluating which method they want to use, they are close to suicidal action. Mental illness and suicide are real problems. Too many teenagers don't make it through the rough years and difficulties.

After my daughter, Lisa, was born, I never rejoined or asked the church for forgiveness. My parents didn't insist. They asked me if I wanted to go and I said no. So, they let it be. Deep down I think they pitied me, standing before that judgmental congregation. Perhaps they believed I had been humiliated and punished enough. It was like a public execution. It was traumatic.

After the ride home from the church meeting, my parents resolved that the eye of the hurricane had passed, and we needed to come out of the valley and prepare for the future. Following my tearful and emotional ride home, my parents snapped out of attack mode.

I was emotionally and psychologically drained from the public church rejection. My parents stopped bemoaning my pregnancy. They went back to focusing on their work. My Mom was the strategist; she started talking to me about the future. I do believe that is the only reason I did not commit suicide before delivery. Mom started talking to me about going to college. She gave me something positive on which to focus. She said, "You can go back to school, finish high school, go to college, try to better yourself. You can pull yourself up. You can still have a good life!" Mom literally became my cheerleader and finally I started thinking the way she was talking. Kudos to my family for shepherding me through the shadow of death. Mom was a miracle worker!

Lisa was born May 24, 1967. Following her birth, my parents became more supportive. Being a teenage mother was a scary endeavor. I didn't have a clue about mothering. I knew little about life – yet here I was responsible for bringing another life into a world that I did not understand. This hit me one day as I was sitting in my room holding Lisa. She was probably three weeks old. I started to feel sorry for this child I had brought into the world. I had nothing to give her. Lisa deserved better than the nothing I had. Thankfully, my oldest sister, Lucille, was out of college and working at the time. She purchased some shoes for Lisa.

My mother helped parent Lisa. Mom did a lot of extra work. God rest her soul. She wanted me to be able to go to class and not be too sleepy, so she took care of Lisa some during the night. In August when school started, Mom made sure I was in school. I had missed a part of the second semester of my junior year. I was nervous about returning to school because I thought children would whisper about me having a baby and being put out of the church. This was 1967 in rural West Tennessee. Mom told me to ignore the gossip and focus on graduating from high school. She said, "If you don't graduate from high school, you'll have problems a lot bigger than what someone says about you." My past classmates were now seniors. I was a junior because I dropped out near the end of my junior year. Thankfully I had earned full credit for the first semester of the junior year.

Prior to the opening of school in August

1967, Mom had gone to the Lauderdale County Superintendent of Schools in Ripley, Tennessee. She told him that it would really benefit me if I could graduate in the summer of 1968 and not have to do another whole year behind my class. She also talked to the Halls High principal. After talking to my Mom, the principal reviewed my record. I had taken some extra high school credits during my freshman and sophomore years. He told my Mom if I would take senior English in the summer of 1968, then I could graduate in August after I finished summer school. Mom rushed home to tell me the good news. She said I could then go to college in September, on time, just like my original freshman classmates. My mom was a strategist. She was the engine. Mom's successful lobbying effort brought me joy – knowing that in a year I could get away from Mt. Zion Church and Halls, Tennessee. Mom told me she and Dad would keep Lisa and I could go on to college. "Try to better yourself, make better decisions, study, apply yourself," she said. Mom was a genius. She had convinced the decision-makers that it was far better to help a child graduate on time than to delay and take a chance that they never graduate.

Mom told me repeatedly, "Don't worry about what people say." Just go and finish high school and go to college on time. Mom stood up for me. She's gone. I can't tell her again. She would go to bat for her kids. Mom would often say, "I'll go through a circle saw while it's turning for my children."

Motherhood changed my life completely. Essentially, motherhood ended my childhood. I missed the usual teen activities. I missed the junior and senior prom. There was no August high school graduation, so I had no high school graduation. I missed some get-togethers, ballgames, and parties. I could never be inducted into the Beta Club because of my pregnancy. I could have forged different relationships and had a different learning experience if I had chosen a different path. I could have enjoyed my high school years.

Teen parenting was hard. It was an extra burden. It was hard to embrace it. I felt somewhat resentful and foolish. I was mostly angry at myself. I remember thinking that I felt sorry for this child. It's unfair to bring children into the world when you're so ill-prepared. So many others have become teen parents – as I did – without even thinking. Most teens can't begin to give children what they need. I was a child when I gave birth and that's problematic. I was still earning spending money by cleaning and babysitting for the Hansfords while my family took care of Lisa.

After Mom successfully planted the seed of me leaving Halls, I felt better. I wanted to make sure I studied and kept up my work so that I could get out of that little town and get a new start. I don't remember going back to that church at all during the year I was finishing high school. I did not ask the church's forgiveness and never asked to rejoin. God forgave me. I felt no need to seek their forgiveness. I did go back to Mt. Zion some years later when I went home. I think it was a Mother's Day program. Mom wanted me to go, and I went to honor her. I never rejoined that church.

My parents enabled me to keep going, make adjustments, and stop wallowing in my mistakes. They said, "It's already done, move on." So, I did, largely due to the support of my family. I don't want to say they didn't have a lot of negative things to say because they were hurt. They were angry. They were shocked. So, early on, they expressed their hurt, disappointment, and anger, but they never deserted me.

My parents continued to go to Mt. Zion Church. That was their church. Mt. Zion was where my Mom grew up – attending church and elementary school there. My Dad had grown up as a Methodist, but when they married and had children, he decided it would be easier if the family attended the same church. Mom wanted to go where her mother went, where her sisters and brothers were, and so forth. That was their church. They remained there; they were loyal members.

When I went back to high school, I don't remember any bad reactions from other students. I don't remember any ugliness. I'm thankful that I don't. I don't remember any girls saying ugly things in the restroom. Maybe they felt sorry for me. Of course, I wasn't the only girl who became pregnant, but it was not as common in 1966 as it is today. I do think different families dealt with it in different ways. For whatever reason, the other students didn't make fun of me and make me feel bad. Neither did the teachers or the administrators. I don't remember anything that made me say, "I don't want to go back to school tomorrow." The school was much kinder to me than the church.

After graduating high school, I would leave to go to college in September 1968 in Nashville at Tennessee Agricultural & Industrial State College just as Mom had promised I could. This was the same year the legislature changed the name to Tennessee State University. The school, since its founding in 1912, was designated as a Historically Black College and University (HBCU).

I couldn't take Lisa to Nashville with me. I had no means. I couldn't rent an apartment, hire a babysitter, and go to school. In fact, I had to work to go to school, so Lisa stayed with my parents. If they had not kept her, I would not have been able to go to college. They couldn't afford to send me to college, but they could afford to keep Lisa and that was their way of helping me. Mom suggested I live with one of my older sisters in Nashville and get a job, work, and go to college. My parents did everything they promised me they would do. They knew Lisa would be in a safe and stable environment living with them. They were wise and they cared.

They did not have money, but they strove to give us the important things – the things that money can't buy – love, respect, togetherness, order, determination, hope, a listening ear, and knowledge that we could stumble and get back up.

Chapter 4

New Horizons, New Life

Crossing the Tennessee River from West to Middle Tennessee was and still is an uplifting experience for me. Rocks in the hillside along Interstate 40 looked like artwork to me. Nashville felt solid, firm and elevated. Nashville still feels that way to me. I love our city and the opportunities it offered. Much needed education and emotional growth happened to me in Nashville. Some of the kindest and most creative people in the world reside here. It thrills me to call Nashville home.

In order to afford college in 1968, I lived with my sister and her husband, Alline and Albert Greer. They were kind and supportive. I had no car. They transported me back and forth to TSU and to work. Albert and I were freshmen at TSU the same year, so I rode with him to school most days. Alline cooked great meals and she also tutored me in Spanish. I deeply appreciate how warmly they took me in when I was homeless. However, I felt that I was imposing on their generosity, so when I met a possible husband, I jumped too quickly.

After settling in with the Greers, I found a job at Sonny's Big Burger that a cousin told me about. I think I was paid about a dollar an hour. Sonny's had a great location on the corner of 18th Avenue North and Jefferson Street. I worked on their busy days – Friday, Saturday, and Sunday – and if they had an opening in the evenings during the week, I would fill in. I worked the grill, made burgers and French fries, cut up onions, tomatoes, lettuce, and made sandwiches. I took orders from customers. A lot of the business was from Fisk University students. Fisk was located immediately across the street. Meharry Medical College was located one block down on the same side as Sonny's restaurant and Tennessee State University (TSU) was about a mile west on Jefferson Street.

In addition to working at Sonny's Big Burger, I also worked part time in the office of Dr. Crawford Lindsey, who was head of the English department at TSU. I did light typing, duplicated tests and other materials and stapled them together for instructors to give to their classes. I ran errands for Dr. Lindsey across campus if he needed some papers dropped off at the Dean's office or the Registrar's office. I answered the phone when the secretary went to lunch, or when she was out. I, like many other poor students, benefited from the university's Work Study

Program.

One day Dr. Lindsey overheard me use hope, h-o-p-e, as a past tense for h-e-l-p. I said to a fellow work study student that she hope me with a task yesterday. Dr. Lindsey asked me to come into his office and told me what he heard me say. He also had noticed that I said ax, a-x, instead of asked, a-s-k-e-d. He explained that ax was a cutting tool, to a-s-k was to make a request. He explained calmly and gently the difference between h-o-p-e and h-e-l-p-e-d. I was embarrassed but grateful that he took his time to teach me things I should have learned in elementary school. Thankfully he talked with me privately.

Dr. Lindsey told me he understood that many of us came to college from very poor school systems. He said his job was to help us improve and that I should study grammar on my own. College instructors, he said, expect students to know certain things when they arrive. Professors will not teach remedial elementary school grammar. It is the student's responsibility to do extra studying to fill in the gaps. I thanked him that day, and I am still to this day most grateful for his honesty and kindness.

I understood that it was my duty to fill in the gaps. All the learning I missed while I was walking from the elementary school to get a head of cabbage to make slaw or to fetch a pint of ice cream for the principal was revealing itself. However, even if I had not gone to the store, the teachers were not teaching basic grammar and math. The educational deficit was mine, as Dr. Lindsey pointed out to me. What Dr. Lindsey said to me was almost identical to what Mrs. Smith said to me in high school. Teachers do not plan to teach elementary school material to high school kids. Now Dr. Lindsey was saying the same about university professors.

The responsibility of filling in my educational gaps was overwhelming to me. I went home and pulled out the Plain English Handbook, copyright 1966, that I was allowed to keep from high school when it was replaced by a newer book. I started to study. I told my oldest sister, Lucille, about Dr. Lindsey's comments. She encouraged me to do the extra studying to fill in the deficits and she volunteered to answer any questions that arose from my extra study. I also remember walking in the park and talking with Lucille about sentence structure and parts of speech. Today the same Plain English Handbook is still in my at-home bookcase.

Being under-educated made me wonder if I could ever graduate from college. There was the extra study needed to overcome the deficit, plus the rigor of ongoing assignments. I also lacked confidence. My boyfriend soon-to-be husband was a high school graduate. James wasn't all that interested in me continuing my college education. All this contributed to my decision to drop out of college in May 1969, after completing my first year. Thinking back, instead of marrying the first person who looked my way, I should have tried to marry a man like Dr. Lindsey – intelligent, well-educated, and cultured who valued higher education.

It was soon after I started working at Sonny's Big Burger restaurant that the owner's brother, James Moses Council, asked me to go to the movies. James was tall (over 6 feet), thin, brown and wore a smile that implied he had life all figured out. He was eleven years older than I. I was eighteen and he was twenty-nine. He had served in the military, and now had a job with the United States Postal Service. We started dating. About nine months later, on June 7, 1969, we got married in the Davidson County Courthouse. No wedding, no reception, no honeymoon. I had no money.

I rushed into marriage, partly because I felt pressure from my Mom. She was afraid I would become pregnant again and have two children out of wedlock. Mom was a nervous wreck. She wanted me to come home for the summer. I did not want to live in Halls and work on the farm during the summer of 1969. I just wanted to calm Mom's anxiety, so marriage seemed like the perfect answer. Jim was older and more experienced, and he had a job, a car, and a small military disability from his time in the service. He had served in Japan and Germany. He had four children from a previous marriage. The children lived with their mother. That meant part of his salary was spent on child support.

James purchased us a house at 3213 Hummingbird Drive in the Treppard Heights subdivision located north of downtown Nashville. He used his VA benefits which allowed him to buy the house with no money down. The purchase price for a well-built all-brick two-bedroom home with a finished basement and one-car garage on a one-acre lot was $17,500 in 1969. It had hardwood floors in the living room and bedrooms.

After I got married in June 1969 and decided to drop out of college, my sister Lucille and her husband Joe Seibert recommended me for a clerical job in the school system in Nashville. At the time, I thought this was the path I needed. Working a clerical job full time was a lot easier than what I had been doing, which was trying to learn what I had missed in elementary and high school and keep up with day-to-day assignments, work at the college and work at Sonny's Big Burger. I wasn't proud of dropping out, but it gave me a chance to catch my breath. I decided it was not a bad life. I felt like I could do the clerical work and it wasn't a big deal. It didn't stress me out like working and going to school. One clerical job and running a household was a piece of cake compared to the rigors of the prior school year. At one point early on, I felt that I could just live this way forever.

I found myself wondering how many other black children from poor segregated school systems dropped out of college because they could not overcome the deficits they inherited from their elementary and high school years. It made me sad and angry. I knew many children in my age group who left college during or after the first year. Some males joined the military and went to the Vietnam War. Some died in the war. How many of us settled for lower paying jobs and lack of funds because of the absence of an adequate public education? A former Lillian Fountain classmate told me that the only job she could get when she moved up North was as a line factory worker because she could never pass the proficiency test the factory required to become a higher-level employee. She stood on her feet in the factory her entire working life; her health suffered as a result. She also said her lifetime earnings were greatly reduced because she could not move up in the company. This impacted the type of housing she could afford and the opportunities she could offer her children. This was caused by the lack of an adequate elementary education.

Even after my 1969 marriage, Lisa continued

living with my parents. They presumed (and they were right) that I still wasn't stable. Nine months after I dropped out of college, on February 22, 1970, I gave birth to Jamie Maria Council, my second daughter. What appeared to be an easy life during the first months of marriage turned out to be the calm before the storm. I was still too immature for motherhood. Postpartum depression enveloped me.

Almost from the beginning of my marriage to Jim, we had problems. I had never felt loneliness until I married him. He went out at night a lot; I was home. He claimed he was working when he wasn't. I would call his job – at this time, he was working as a clerk at United Parcel Service – and they would say he's not here or he didn't work today. He lied to me a lot.

The rejection from Jim, coupled with the loneliness and twenty-four/seven responsibility for Jamie drove me into a deep depression. I was a college dropout with two young children and a husband who was a gambler and womanizer. Thoughts of suicide returned to me – thoughts I had not had since the teen pregnancy. Ugly negative thoughts flooded my consciousness: I am a failure, why not admit it and give up? I've disgraced my family. I was de-churched. I don't even have a solid elementary education. I can't speak like college students.

I didn't study when I should have. Instead, I was out getting pregnant. Four sisters ahead of me are college grads. My brothers are model students. My parents are rearing my child. These thoughts went on and on and on. Hell reigned in my head.

I remember one particularly gloomy day in the midst of these thoughts. I took Jamie to her granny's, Jim's mother. Granny was a sweet and gentle lady who worshipped her son Jim. I called my work and told them I was not coming in because I was sick. I returned home trying to decide how to end my life of failures and rejections. I sat on the ground in the backyard with my heavy thoughts. I considered several methods. I decided I would go to the doctor and ask for sleeping pills and then just take an overdose. I knew my family would take care of my girls.

Immediately after I decided how I would end my life, a strange dog came across the ditch and started barking at me. I had never seen the dog before. I got up and backed away. He advanced. As I reached for a stick on the ground, the dog came closer. I struck at him. He stood there and barked. I swung again and he chased me into the house. That incident somehow energized me.

When I entered the house, the phone was ringing. Cell phones did not exist in 1970. If the dog had not chased me into the house, I would have missed this call. My sister Rose had called me at work. They told her I was not there. Rose said, "If you're sick, what's wrong?" I started to tell her some of my thoughts. I didn't tell her I considered suicide, but I told her I felt that I had messed up by life. She listened quietly as I described all the mistakes I had made. I vented. I poured out my soul – I told her I was a pitiful failure. When I finally stopped talking, Rose assured me that everything would be alright. "Life has its ups and downs. You're experiencing a downward slope. You'll be just fine," Rose said. That conversation was therapy for me that day when I needed it the most.

After talking to Rose, my appetite returned. I got something to eat, and I started to feel a lot better. My appetite had been terrible in the days prior. Rose helped me understand that it is not always easy to transition from being a child to being a young adult. In 1970, Rose helped me see that I was a normal person going through one of life's valleys. I never considered suicide again.

Any person experiencing suicidal thoughts now can call 9-8-8 for help. This resource was not available in years past.

Back to College

Even though Joe Seibert (my sister Lucille's husband who is now deceased) was instrumental in getting me the clerical job with Metro Public Schools, Lucille and Joe reminded me gently, but constantly, that I needed to go back to college. Of course, Jim didn't like that idea, but I decided in 1971 to attend Meharry Medical College, seeking a diploma in dental hygiene. It was a two-year program. Joe's sister Wilda was a dental hygienist and she worked at a federal clinic in north Nashville that catered to poor people. The dental clinic was part of the Matthew Walker Health Center. If I could get a job like that, then maybe my family would stop talking to me about college. Dental hygienists are professionals; they earn a decent salary. I needed to make more money. Clerical work did not pay well. If I could become a dental hygienist in two years, then maybe I could support my children in a better way.

Meharry Medical College is a historically black medical school affiliated with the United Methodist Church. It was founded in 1876, eleven years after the end of the Civil War "with the mission of educating African Americans to serve the underserved," according to the college. Meharry is a beacon for a lot of people. Many black people who practice medicine or dentistry in America are graduates of Meharry. I was happy to be enrolled there.

I found both black and white faculty members who were knowledgeable and caring people. The hygiene class included six blacks and five whites. One day, when we were all waiting for the teacher, classmates started discussing their grades from the last test. I announced my grade, which was fairly high. Doris, a white girl who drove up from Alabama to class everyday stated with a big smile, "Jannie you're a golden nigger." All of us in the room that day were shocked. Blacks in alphabetical order were Pamela Butler, Jannie Council, Gennette Davis, Lynda Hawthorne, Carolyn Johnson and Beverly Robbins. White students were Doris Alldredge, Wanda Fuqua, Kathleen Jones, June Proctor and Marion Setzer.

My classmates, both black and white, started to chastise Doris. One black classmate said to Doris, "I should just slap you right now." A white classmate scolded Doris saying, "You might get us all put out of this black school. What are you thinking?" Doris hastened to explain that she intended that statement as a compliment to me. She thought she was saying something nice. She explained "That's what we call black people we like in Alabama."

Doris went on to explain the "compliment" she had just given me. She said it had something to do with being worth our weight in gold, thus "golden nigger." When Doris explained that she meant it as a compliment, she looked perplexed. Doris didn't understand why we were so upset. She had used that language all her life; this was part of her culture. Doris seemed oblivious to the idea that relating blacks to gold was a cruel reminder that we had been bought and sold like cattle. Classmates gave Doris a crash course in race relations. Doris was enrolled in a predominantly black institution sitting in a classroom study session surrounded by blacks. She thought she was giving me a compliment. This was 1971!

Of course, the girls in class told other people. When Mrs. Chandler, the director of the dental hygiene program, heard about this incident, she met with each of us privately, then with both of us. Doris apologized to me. We moved on. The other blacks largely ignored Doris after that incident. I was busy trying to learn all the things I needed to know. I was still busy trying to fill in my learning gaps from earlier in my life. I needed to graduate and feed my two kids. I let it go. But the incident spread over the college like wildfire. The medical and dental students started calling me "Superstar" after this incident. I believe it was their way of lifting me up emotionally and showing their support.

A white professor talked to me after he heard what Doris had said. He explained to me that racial ignorance was rampant. He thanked me for not making a bigger deal about this. He said perhaps Doris was surprised that I could learn quicker than she and some other classmates. He told me I was more intelligent than Doris and I possessed an excellent mind. "Use your brain to focus on your goals and you will meet with overwhelming success," he said. This conversation was a confidence booster for me. He cared enough to encourage me. He predicted I would be successful. I wish I could recall his name. Following the "golden nigger" incident, I felt additional support from administrators, professors, medical, dental, and dental hygiene students. Meharry Medical College is an international, national and Nashville treasure.

Classes at Meharry were challenging. Head and neck anatomy was difficult for me. Dr. James Pulliam, a black instructor, taught this class. He was a short, light-skinned man who wore a winter hat with earmuffs. Everyone knew Dr. Pulliam by his hat. His favorite cap was red, sometimes one earflap was up and one was down. He had a big smile that showed his wide front teeth. He spoke rather softly and his eyes showed kindness. He was willing to meet for extra sessions for anyone who needed extra help. Dr. Pulliam gave hours of his personal time to help students learn.

There was so much to learn about the head and neck. This was more difficult for me because I had never had a real biology course. I was lost. Dr. Pulliam came to special extra sessions equipped with a model of the human skull. He said this was the foundation of what we needed to understand. Dr. Pulliam taught us head and neck anatomy. He pointed out the openings, sinuses, canals, eye sockets, maxilla and mandible (the upper and lower jaw respectively.) Pay extra attention to the mandible and maxilla, he said, as your career will be spent largely on these two bones. Dr. Pulliam pointed out the major features of the skull. Slowly, I started to gain a bit of confidence.

During some sessions, he asked us to take turns identifying various anatomical features. By observing, listening, discussing, and asking questions we learned head and neck anatomy. Once we articulated some understanding of the skull, Dr. Pulliam moved on to the brain, medulla oblongata, spinal cord, and nerves. He then discussed the orifices through which the nerves and blood vessels traveled. Dr. Pulliam spent quite a bit of time teaching about the trigeminal nerve because it is responsible for sending pain, touch, and temperature sensations from the face to the brain. He helped me appreciate how truly amazing the human body is – intricate, sensitive, automated, self-repairing and marvelously engineered. Dr. Pulliam's instruction provided the class a new level of confidence.

Requirements for becoming a registered dental hygienist were similar to those for becoming a registered nurse. Our class understood that we had to pass all course work, and pass a practical and written state exam in addition to a written national board exam. We studied with all these requirements in mind.

When I took the national board examination and specific questions were asked, I could recall Dr. Pulliam's explanations and examples. I could see him pointing to the trigeminal nerve and other anatomical landmarks on his chart. His instruction helped me score an 89 on the national board. There were many great instructors at Meharry who helped dental, medical and allied health students. Confines of space will not allow me to acknowledge all of them here. Highlighting Dr. Pulliam allows me to show the level of dedicated and caring professors I encountered at Meharry. This instruction showed me that a teacher's ability to meet a student at the student's level and move the student forward through careful guided instruction is the mark of a master teacher. Dr. Pulliam was a master teacher.

When I was ready to graduate from dental hygiene, Dr. Pulliam encouraged me to go on to dental school. I thanked him for the vote of confidence, but explained my deficits, especially in math. Dr. Pulliam gave me a handheld calculator the next day. He said, keep this in your purse and it will boost your confidence. It did. I kept it in my purse for years. Nine years later the calculator helped me pass the real estate exam. In a very real sense, Meharry provided me a life uplifting experience. I had never participated in a graduation prior to Meharry's graduation. More importantly, the Meharry experience showed me that I could study and learn.

I graduated from Meharry Medical College on May 27, 1973, with a diploma in dental hygiene. My graduating class included six blacks and five whites. Even though I scored 89 on the national board exam and performed well on the Tennessee Board of Dentistry practical exam – I showed that I could clean teeth (oral prophylaxis), take x-rays and perform oral exams – I could not get a job in Nashville in 1973 because I was black. I was the only black hygiene graduate who lived in Nashville. The other blacks went home to places like Los Angeles, Chicago and Detroit.

My classmate, the girl I studied with during the two years of dental hygiene school, was offered several hygienist jobs with good salaries. She was an attractive Italian girl. I scored higher on the national exam than she. She thought it was horrible that I couldn't get a job. She asked a couple of white dentists that she knew to hire me, but they did not. It depressed me for a while. I had two children and expenses.

So, I again went to work as a secretary, this

time doing clerical work at Metropolitan Nashville and Davidson County Model Cities program. Model Cities was funded by the Federal government.

Again, my sister Lucille urged me to get a college degree. I resisted at first, feeling that maybe that would not help me either. She assured me that she and her husband worked in the Metro Nashville Public School system, and they could help me get a teaching job. So, I started taking night classes in 1974 at the University of Tennessee (UT). In 1974, UT Nashville was a predominantly white school located at 10th Avenue North and Charlotte in the downtown area. The campus is now TSU Downtown.

UT was well operated and organized. I could register for the quarter and buy books during one lunch hour. Since I worked a clerical job the entire time I attended UT, this was a major convenience. Teachers taught; however, it wasn't at all like Meharry. I felt overlooked, left out and insignificant at UT.

My white male psychology teacher, Dr. Cozy, somehow detected my inner-feelings and state of mind and asked me to stop by his office. He said to me, "You have as much right to be here as any other student. You are a bright student. You have as much right to be in America as anyone else. Don't apologize for being black, for being in a mostly white environment." I thought, wow, he saw me. Somehow, he had detected my repressed feelings; he had observed my behavior. That talk caused me to stop tiptoeing around white people and to speak up in class. It gave me confidence and hope. I struggled to earn decent grades while working a job and being a Mom to Jamie.

My siblings (Lucille, Dennis and William Jr.) babysat Jamie as needed and tutored me. I remember my brothers put up a chalk board and helped me with things I should have known but I didn't know. William Jr. attended the integrated school system from eighth grade through high school. Dennis attended from sixth grade through high school. They had a solid elementary education. They never laughed at me, judged me, or made me feel stupid. They just filled in the gaps. Lucille tutored me in basic grammar and writing. Sometimes I carried Jamie to the UT nursery while I attended night classes. Sometimes I would pick up Dennis from TSU baseball team practice and he would babysit. During my three years as a UT college student, Lucille, my brother Dennis, and the UT Nursery looked after Jamie while I attended night classes. Jamie's father did not babysit. When I took Jamie from day care to UT evening care, I would stop at UT's cafeteria and get her a honeybun and chocolate milk. She loved it!

My day job at the Model Cities grant program ended in 1975. Lucille and Joe recommended me to their church pastor who needed a part-time secretary. Rev. Michael Lee Graves pastored Pilgrim Emanuel Baptist Church at the corner of 10th Avenue South and Douglas Streets. He hired me and I worked for him at the church office. Rev. Graves was kind, respectful and caring. He was a true scholar. Rev. Graves encouraged me to complete my college education. He was an excellent boss, a loving husband to his wife Eleanor, an attentive father, and a good human being.

On June 6, 1977, I was awarded a Bachelor of Science Degree in Education from the University of Tennessee. I started looking for an entry level professional job, and true to my sister's promise, I was offered a teaching position at the school where I did my student teaching under Ms. Erma J. Todd, my sister's dear friend.

Ms. Todd gave me a favorable student teacher evaluation and recommended me to the principal. My brother-in-law Joe, who worked at the Board of Education office, put in a good word for me. Joe was friendly and likable. Joe knew all the decision-makers at the Central Office. Ms. Todd had recommended me to Mr. Stanfill at John Overton High School, and he wanted to hire me. I was extremely grateful that Lucille and Joe had encouraged me to complete my undergraduate degree.

I had also heard that the Metro Nashville Health Department was going to hire a dental hygienist. So, I applied to both the health department and the school system. The school system offered me a job teaching freshman English at Overton High School. They called me on the morning of Thursday, August 11, 1977. I immediately said yes. The health department offered me a job as a dental hygienist that same afternoon. I accepted the health department's job because it paid a little more. Also, I had doubts as to whether I could control twenty-five to thirty students all day and help them learn in a meaningful way. I explained and apologized to Ms. Todd, Joe, and Lucille. They understood. Lucille and Joe Seibert kept every promise they made to me. They never gave up on me. They looked out for me. I shall always be deeply grateful for their guidance, support, and love.

After I accepted the dental hygienist job, Mrs. Elsa Chandler asked me to stop by her office. She was director of Meharry's Dental Hygiene Program. She said Dr. B, who was Director of the Metro Nashville Health Department, had intended to pay me less than the established pay scale because I was black. The health department had never hired a black dental hygienist, and he felt that he was taking a risk. Mrs. Chandler advised Dr. B against this. She told him she would not quietly condone this blatant salary discrimination – nor would she advise me to do so. She told him her program trained black and white students the same way, same skill set, same national boards, same state of Tennessee practical examination. "All black hygienists deserve the same pay as white hygienists," she said. Mrs. Chandler, a black woman who grew up on the East coast of the United States, was well-educated, cultured, highly respected, and well-spoken. She stood up for her students.

Mrs. Chandler never told me how she found out about Dr. B's desire to pay me less. Perhaps he called and talked to her. Mrs. Chandler advised me to become a good employee, go to work early, be cooperative and learn quickly how Metro's system worked. She encouraged me to stay in touch if I needed her help. She said I would do well. I thanked her profusely. She asked that I not discuss this with anyone else. I did not. This happened mid-August of 1977.

I returned to my car that day, rolled the windows down, put my head on the steering wheel and cried. Dr. B clearly preferred a white dental hygienist. However, the city's pay scale did not allow him to pay them the amount of money they were all making in private practices. The only reason I got an interview, as Mrs. Chandler said, was that I was qualified. I deserved as much pay as a white girl with the same degree. I had a dental hygiene diploma and a Bachelor of Science Degree in Education. I was more qualified than the white girls with a two-year dental hygiene diploma, yet Dr. B wanted to pay me less.

I wept that day, not just for me, but for all black people who are mistreated every day in so many ways. I thought about how easy job hunting had gone for my white classmates. Kathleen went to work for her brother-in-law who was a dentist. June, Wanda, and Marian had several job offers, and all had been gainfully employed since we graduated in 1973. Doris went home to Alabama where jobs awaited. Four years after graduation, I was still facing job discrimination. At this point in 1977, I had already been robbed (because I was black) of four years of higher earnings. I should have been able to get a job as a dental hygienist when I graduated in 1973.

I had tried back in 1973 to find a job with a black dentist, but most of them couldn't afford a full-time dental hygienist. Many black dentists at that time worked for Meharry, the prison system or Veterans Administration full time, and only worked part time in the evenings at their private practice. They would typically look for a part-time dental hygienist, or they would clean the teeth themselves and hire only a dental assistant.

When I was looking for a job at white dentists' offices, I could tell they weren't going to hire me even as I talked to the receptionists. When I said to them, "Do you have any dental hygiene jobs open?" they would look at me like, you think he's going to hire you? They gave me that kind of once up-and-down look. I didn't beat the bushes and I didn't knock on the door of every white dental practice, but the fact that Dr. B was hesitant to hire me in public health speaks to the depth of racism and discrimination in 1977 in Nashville and in the South. The health department received federal dollars, yet he was hesitant about hiring the first ever black dental hygienist in Metro Nashville. He only approved the hiring because there were no white applicants. They were all working and earning more, but Dr. B wanted to pay me less because I was black. This felt like a curse.

I decided to follow Mrs. Chandler's advice to keep quiet, watch my back and be the best dental hygienist I could be. The Metro Health personnel director told me I would be starting at step one for a dental hygienist at the salary I had been promised.

Most of the patients didn't care that I was black. There was one who did. I called his name in the waiting area, and he came in and took a seat in the dental chair. Apparently, he thought I was the dental assistant and that I was going to get the dental hygienist. So, when he found out I was the hygienist, he said something like "You gonna' work on my mouth?" I said, "Yes, I'm going to clean your teeth." He started unbuckling the bib from his neck that holds the cloth on the chest, and he said, "I don't want my teeth cleaned that bad." He just got up and walked out. That was the most direct rejection I encountered as a dental hygienist.

Most of my patients, black women and white women with children, and immigrant families, seemed happy to have someone to examine, clean and apply fluoride to their children's teeth. They did not care that I was black. There were never any complaints about my job performance.

I found most of my co-workers supportive. The dental assistants, one was black and one white, got along well with me. If I wasn't busy, I would help them out, so we started to work as a team. I got along with everybody. Several caring and knowledgeable public health workers became my lifelong friends.

My marriage continued to limp along. I felt trapped because I didn't feel that I could divorce Jim, stand on my own and support my children. Being married to Jim really caused me to want to take total control of my finances. He always wanted to make all the decisions. He handled or mismanaged all our earnings. He was very controlling. I think he felt like he could get away with it because I was eleven years younger than he. It became a real issue for me.

I worked, got paid and Jim gave me a small allowance – like a child. Many days I took my lunch to work so I could stretch my allowance. Jim and I had agreed to save my salary. I put my check in savings on the 7th and 22nd of each month. Those were Metro paydays. I lived within the allowance Jim gave me. I saved my entire check, but the savings would dissipate.

About every six months I would ask Jim, "How much do we have in savings now?" He would say, well, I had to use some for tires and some clothes or something. In reality, he was renting motel rooms and taking women out, buying gifts and gambling and whatever else. The money we saved evaporated. Something was really wrong here. I realized I needed to balance my own checkbook. I needed to know where the money was going. There was no way to ever attain my childhood goal of financial independence as long as Jim managed my money.

On Saturday, July 8, 1978, at approximately 3:35 p.m., I saw Jim with his girlfriend at the Gulf gas station across from the Amoco station off I-40 East. The girlfriend seemed quite happy as she jumped out of his yellow Cadillac to smile and chat with him as he pumped gas. She wore tightly fitting blue jeans and a light blue top. She was slightly heavy with a curly hair style. Lisa was vacationing with us. I was taking Jamie and Lisa to Opryland (a music themed amusement park that was open in Nashville back then). Jim had told me he had to work in Chattanooga, so he would be out of town over the weekend. When I saw them, I had thoughts of crashing my car into his and trying to hurt both of them, but it would have injured us as well. My children would have been traumatized both physically and emotionally. They never saw Jim across the street, and I did not tell them. They were excited about spending the day at Opryland. I'm glad I did not spoil their fun. They enjoyed Opryland. I was inwardly angry at the lies and betrayal of my husband. However, I compartmentalized my feelings that day and pretended to be happy for my children's sake. My children deserved some happiness, and they always enjoyed the rides and musical shows.

I knew from that day forward that I should manage my income and make sure my check was not being used to rent hotel rooms for Jim and his women. I was saving my check each month, spending only the allowance he gave me and here he was living it up with his woman. I was very angry and hurt. If Jamie and Lisa had not been with me,

I would have crashed my little inexpensive Ford into his big yellow Cadillac. I probably would have landed in jail. However, being a Mom required me to swallow the notion of violence and act like a responsible adult.

On that day, I decided to divorce Jim at my first available opportunity, but I would only do it when it became clear to me that I could provide adequately for myself and my children, when I could stand on my own financially.

Jannie's maternal grandparents, Louis and
Beulah Sawyer Hudson, (Mama Beulah and Daddy Louis).

Jannie's paternal grandparents, left to right, Janie Claybrooks Carter
(Mama Janie) and Anderson Charles Carter (Papa), and
Missy Carter, Papa's daughter from a prior marriage.

William and Luella Hudson Carter,
Jannie's parents.

Jannie Olevia Carter, about 11 months old, in 1951.
The family's home in the background reveals the
poverty into which she was born.

Jannie's four brothers, left to right, William Jr., Dennis Charles,
Cleo, and Kenneth Bernard Carter. About 1963.

Lillian Fountain Grammar School where Jannie attended grades 1 through 8.
Note the word 'Grammar' on the sign is misspelled as 'Grammer'.
Jannie says, "If authorities did not know enough or care enough to spell the name of
the school correctly, imagine the lack of teaching that occurred inside."

Jannie and her five sisters and parents. Left to right, Geraldine, Willie Mae, Rose Marie, William Carter, Sr., Luella, Alline, Jannie Olevia, and Lucille.

Mt. Zion Missionary Baptist Church. Jannie was
expelled from Mt. Zion in 1967.

The Carter Family at the celebration of Mama Luella's GED
Graduation in 1992. From left to right, front row: Rose Ballard,
Alline Greer, Lucille Seibert, William Carter, Sr., Luella Carter,
Geraldine Pitts, and Willie Mae Graham. Back row: Dennis Charles,
William Jr., Jannie, Cleo, and Kenneth Bernard Carter.
Photo by Neal Ammons.

Left to right: Lisa Carter (Jannie's daughter), Jannie,
Jamie Sawyer (daughter) and Jacob Carter Sawyer
(Jannie's grandson).

The Carter family home and farm
in the background.

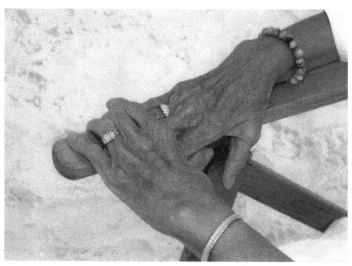

Jannie's mother's hands at age 90 in 2012.

THE METROPOLITAN GOVERNMENT OF NASHVILLE AND DAVIDSON COUNTY

STATEMENT OF EARNINGS AND DEDUCTIONS

674831

EMPLOYEE NAME	FUND	ACCOUNT NO	EMP NO	SOCIAL SECURITY NO.	PERIOD ENDING
JANNIE C. COUNCIL	114	599.133	185036		04/15/75

REGULAR HOURS	GROSS	FEDERAL INCOME TAX YEAR TO DATE	F I C A YEAR TO DATE	PENSION	BOND BALANCE	
	343.00	39.94	10.29			
OVERTIME HOURS	YEAR TO DATE	YEAR TO DATE	CUMULATIVE	BOND PURCHASED	NET PAY
	2,744.00	319.52	160.56	260.62	$****264.13
					*ADJUSTMENT

LIFE	HOSP	U.G.F.
2.66	4.03	1.88

*A - ADDITIONAL PAY D - DOCKED AMOUNT U - UNDER PAYMENT O - OVER PAYMENT

A paystub in 1975 shows Jannie's net pay, on the 15th and 30th of each month, was $264.13, which totaled $528.26 per month or $6,339.12 per year.

101 501 021 00

2 Employer's name, address, and ZIP code

18503

METROPOLITAN GOV'T OF NASHVILLE
AND DAVIDSON COUNTY
PAYROLL SUPERVISOR
NASHVILLE, TENN. 37201
690630455

8 Employee's social security number

12 Employee's name address and ZIP code

JANNIE C. GRAY

3816 DUNBAR DR
NASHVILLE   TN
                             37207

Form W-2 Wage and Tax Statement 1987

Copy B To be filed with employee's FEDERAL tax return

OMB No. 1545-0008

3 Employer's identification number	4 Employer's state I.D. number
62-0694743	

5 Statutory employee	Deceased	Pension plan X	Legal rep	942 emp	Deferred compensation

6 Allocated tips	7 Advance EIC payment

10 Wages, tips, other compensation	11 Social security tax withheld
32,370.80	2,314.52

13 Social security wages	14 Social security tips
32,370.80	

16	16a Fringe benefits incl. in Box 10

17 State income tax	18 State wages, tips, etc.	19 Name of state
20 Local income tax	21 Local wages, tips, etc.	22 Name of locality

9 Federal income tax withheld

3,989.50

This information is being furnished to the Internal Revenue Service.

Dept of the Treasury I.R.S.
IRS App.   31-0455-40

In 1987, Jannie earned $32,370.80 as a dental hygienist.

Jannie's parents' gravesite and tombstone.

Part II

Chapter 5

'It Seemed Like a Logical Choice'

In 1982, Jannie's fifth year working full time as a dental hygienist at the Metro Health Department in Nashville, she decided it was time to fulfill a longtime goal: work a second job to help her become financially independent. As a young adult, she read about this idea and it was at that time she told herself she would one day figure out how the economy worked, become productive in business and make sure she was never again poor. She always remembered her parents' financial struggles. Jannie wanted to rise above that.

In her research to determine the best path, she read several books that indicated there were more millionaires created from real estate ownership than from any other business. Jannie's study convinced her that real estate offered the best possibility for financial success. She studied several years before she had any money to invest.

"It seemed like something that maybe I could do," Jannie says. "I couldn't buy oil wells or buy expensive commercial businesses, but I could maybe buy a piece of real estate or sell real estate and create some extra income. It seemed like a logical choice."

Her initial goals were to create a substantial second income and get on solid financial footing so she could end what she described as a "non-working, dysfunctional" thirteen-year marriage to Jim.

"He was not allowing me to be in charge of, or control, how I spent my own income. I was also really thinking about my two children, Lisa and Jamie. I wanted them to go to college, and not have a lot of debt. I didn't want them to have to work at a Sonny's Big Burger like I had to do to help pay for college."

The reality that she wasn't going to become financially independent working as a dental hygienist was reinforced when she received a $68 a month raise on May 22, 1982.

To work in real estate, she needed to take classes and pass an exam to get her Tennessee real estate license. Jim did not want her to become a Realtor, she says, "probably because he knew I was not going to share the income I would make and he wouldn't have as much control over me."

To attend six weeks of classes at a private real estate school meant she needed to go several nights a week and on Saturdays. But having studied at the University of Tennessee Nashville downtown campus (later changed to Tennessee State University) and having been a part-time student working toward an undergraduate degree prepared her for real estate classes.

"Several students in the real estate class were saying this was really hard, and that it was too much working full time and then coming to class at night. But to me it was like a walk in the park," Jannie recalls. "I had taken twelve hours of college credits and worked a secretarial job, so this seemed like no problem. For me, it was equivalent to taking one college course."

Even the math calculations that are a necessary part of real estate didn't seem particularly difficult, although Jannie considered math to be her weakest area. The instructor, though, taught a method to help students come up with math answers somewhat easily.

Jannie studied during her lunch hour at her job as a dental hygienist. She read Tennessee real estate laws and at the end of the six weeks, she felt ready to take the real estate exam, which was on Saturday, August 28, 1982, at UT's downtown campus.

"This seemed quite normal to me to take an exam at UT. I felt well-prepared, and after the approximately three-hour exam, I felt like I had passed. I remember thinking I knew most of the material. Once again, a good teacher made a positive difference for me."

Jannie wrote in her diary that it was 12:25 p.m. on September 14, 1982, when she called the Tennessee Real Estate Commission and was told that she had passed the exam.

"I was elated. The next day, September 15, I went to a photographer to get pictures for my business card." In her daily calendar, she wrote: "I feel good about my future. If I work hard, I might make it."

She signed on as an agent at Century 21 Voss Realtors in Green Hills. Voss conducted frequent training sessions in the evenings. She also traveled to Century 21's training session in Alabama. "I left the training feeling really fired up and energized."

She began asking friends and family to refer clients to her. She also made cold-calls during training at the office, but like many salespeople, she didn't feel comfortable doing that. She got no clients from cold calling people or from people who came into the real estate office.

Some Realtors market their services by concentrating on an area or group of neighborhoods and "farm" it as it's called. That means frequently distributing information to homeowners and getting to know them so they would recognize you as the Realtor to call if they wanted to sell their home. Jannie's broker told her that her "farm" could be her friends and family. She just needed to be diligent about continually reminding them she's in the real estate business and ask them to let others know.

"I started off well," she says. "There was hardly a free moment for me. I had two jobs, two children, one husband. Both dental hygiene and real estate came with required continuing education courses, so I was one big juggling act. I learned a lot during 1982."

Wherever leads came from, Jannie worked with sellers, listing their homes, and she worked with buyers, including a relative who bought a condo. She also talked to close friends at work and word spread that she was a Realtor. She showed some property to a young dentist and his wife.

"Although I showed several houses to them, he later told me they were going to build a house and they would no longer need my help. He was very polite, and I was a little bit let down at first and discouraged. I kind of wondered – is this the way things are going to go? But it dawned on me that I had gained a lot of experience showing them property. I learned how to set up property showings. I learned how to handle objections. It all gave me experience that was really, really helpful. I didn't have time to mope about it anyway. That's the way real estate sales work. Not everybody you work with is going to end up buying or selling."

Soon, a friend referred a couple planning to sell their house. So, Jannie listed it.

"Things just started to take off," she says.

Jannie worked with blacks and whites. "Most people were polite, but sometimes you could sense that the sellers weren't happy that a black agent and client were walking through their home." A few sellers seemed to watch the prospective buyers' every move.

One time she was showing houses to a couple – a friend and her husband, both of whom are black. The couple decided on a house in Brentwood, an upscale area of Nashville. Jannie wrote the contract with the couple's offer, which was very low, but Jannie was legally obligated to present it. So, with her friends in the car, she drove to the home of the listing agent.

Jannie recalls the agent came out on the porch, looked at the offer, and said, "Why would you bring me this niggardly offer?"

"I had never heard 'niggardly' used that way," Jannie says. She said, "Why would you even bother to bring this to me? I'd buy it myself before I sell it to y'all for this." Niggardly, in fact, means not generous or stingy. "The agent chose that adjective intentionally. I felt she meant it as a put-down; it did open my eyes to the fact that I have to really look at the comparable sales and help clients understand comps so they can expect that a lowball offer is likely to be rejected.

"People back then weren't accustomed to black real estate agents like they are now. There weren't that many of us around," Jannie said.

Although most of Jannie's listings of homes for sale were owned by blacks, she also listed properties of whites. "What I came to understand is once people get to know you, then race is not a huge issue-- not as looming. That's what I experienced."

Still, she felt racism often lurked beneath the surface.

"We can't deny racism exists because certainly it does," Jannie says. "But I realized that it's a part of life; it's a part of the real world. It is possible to acknowledge that racism is real and present and continue to move forward. History, knowledge, and patience have helped me manage racism, remain diligent, be aware, take positive action where possible, never lose hope, never give up, and be open and kind to the good people of all races who strive to make the world a better place."

On December 1, 1982, Jannie's husband Jim said he might be transferred in his job. He suggested she would probably want to stop selling real estate. The transfer didn't happen, but even if it had, Jannie says she had no intention of quitting her work as a Realtor. She was just getting started on her goal of becoming financially independent by working a second job.

Her days were jammed as a result of working as a dental hygienist and Realtor. Reading her calendar, she noted a typical day. "On Tuesday, December 28, 1982, I worked from 8:00 a.m. to 4:30 p.m. I was tired from serving dinner to my extended family on December 27, which was a post-holiday gathering at my house. During my lunch hour, I took a contract to Ruby, a client whose house I had listed. Because I was a new agent, my broker helped me fill out the form properly. After work, I picked up a contract at another real estate office for another of my clients, my brother Cleo and his wife. I delivered Ruby's contract to another office, and I took a copy of Cleo and Renee's contract to them. At the end of the day, I was exhausted. I was always getting home late. My daughter Jamie spent a lot of time with her paternal grandmother, whom she called Granny. I would pick her up when I was finished, and then I'd take the fairly long drive home. The next morning, I would start all over again. Some days it was like having two full-time jobs."

When Jamie was out of school or she spent the night with relatives, Jannie would go to work at the health department early to clean dental instruments or restock supplies, or to be there when patients came early. "I did this, really, to show I was devoted to my day job. I never wanted my bosses to think I was short-changing my work with Metro Public Health Department. I gained a reputation of being a hard worker, and I maintained that reputation."

Working two jobs during the last quarter of 1982 into 1983, Jannie was disciplined financially. She didn't buy clothes, household goods or other items on credit. Interest rates at the time were very high. If she needed something for her house, she would pay cash. She also continually reminded herself of the importance of saving. "I would place little notes on my mirror: 'Save' and 'Save as much as possible.'"

Saving money whenever and wherever she could was helpful. And, even though she felt she wasn't yet getting ahead financially, she still believed that working in real estate would ultimately pay off.

Interest on real estate mortgages in the early to mid-1980s was at times 12 to 15 percent or more, but people were still buying, Jannie says. "I was fortunate and blessed. We used to dream about what it would be like if rates ever got back to 10 percent. We thought that would be wonderful."

During 1983, Jannie's first full year in real estate, she was doing very well. "My confidence continued to build because I remember my broker saying, at the rate you're closing, you're doing better than most of my full-time agents. He had only one full-time agent who was ahead of me in closings. I felt really good about that."

Working with sellers and buyers, she finished the year with 18 closings.

Jannie considered leaving her job at the health department and working full time in real estate, but she was concerned about what would happen if her sales slowed.

"If I'm living solely on commissions, where does that leave my children? If I had just been responsible for myself, I think I would have left my dental hygienist job, but I was concerned about providing for my children and I felt like they deserved to go to college."

She also didn't believe she had saved enough money or was on strong enough financial footing to end her marriage, which she still planned to do.

In almost any type of sales job, especially one where the person's income is dependent solely on commissions, most salespeople believe that attitude and mental stamina can be as important as sales skills. For Jannie, one source of inspiration came from a well-known poem, *Desiderata*, written in 1927 by Max Ehrmann.

Jannie's friend, Joan Seigenthaler, who was a manager at the health department, had given Jannie a copy of the poem after the two of them were talking one day. "I said to Joan that all my siblings would be more successful than I. Like me, she was born into a large family. Joan said to me, 'You shouldn't compare yourself to other people.' No one had told me that before.

"I read *Desiderata* and I was blown away. It has made a lot of difference in how I live and how I deal with other people. I shared it with most people in my family because I do think families, and good friends, ought to share things that are helpful. I shared it with other people in the health department, as well. I said to my youngest brother, I learned more from what Joan gave me on one sheet of paper than I learned from all the sermons I had to sit through as a child. It's just amazing."

One part of the poem Joan referred to was: "If you compare yourself to others you may become vain and bitter, for always there will be greater and lesser persons than yourself." Jannie says that message made a huge difference to her, as did another one from the poem: "Beyond a wholesome discipline, be gentle with yourself."

"I was so hard on myself for obvious reasons. I had made not-so-good decisions early in my life and in my marriage. I think Joan sensed that this poem would help. That was so kind of her.

"The framed poem hangs in my hallway. I

revisit it frequently. It says '...it's still a beautiful world. Be cheerful. Strive to be happy. ...be at peace with God, whatever you conceive Him to be." It has helped me a lot with living life fully and conducting business.

"Sometimes you work with clients for several months and then they end up doing something else, or back then, people would meet an agent at an open house and do business with them. I like the part of the poem that says 'nurture the strength of spirit to shield you in sudden misfortune,' and 'enjoy your achievements as well as your plans. Keep interested in your own career, however humble; it is a real possession in the changing fortunes of time. Exercise caution in your business affairs for the world is full of trickery. But let this not blind you to what virtue there is; many persons strive for high ideals, and everywhere life is full of heroism. Be yourself. Especially do not feign affection. Neither be cynical about love.'

"To me, the poem addresses the whole person. It's a condensed life philosophy."

Jannie also did a lot of reading – self-help books that provided advice and guidance in life and business. In 1982, in her calendar, she wrote under the heading Notes for Next Year: "Strengthening the will to win." This, she says, probably came from a book she was reading at the time.

"Number one was increase awareness of where you are, that is, your situation," she says. "Number two, increase the awareness of where you want to go, that is, of achieving your goal. Three, let go of internal interferences: fears, doubts, concepts. Four, give up unnecessary objectives, seek active inspiration from those of like commitment. Number five, practice frequently and with awareness."

Number four – give up unnecessary objectives – helped her to narrow her major goals to two, she says. "Because I worked in public health, I saw how so many black people were obese or overweight; obesity leads to all kinds of health issues. So, I decided I wanted to maintain my ideal weight over my lifetime, and I wanted to secure financial independence. Those were the two goals I selected. I just held to them and focused on them."

That time period, she says, was "really a turning point for me."

Among the books she read then was one related to finances. She doesn't recall the title, but the book's message was to save and invest 15 percent of what you make as a way to help create financial security for yourself. Other books she read later on included *The Millionaire Next Door* and Stephen Covey's *The 7 Habits of Highly Effective People*.

Reunion

In 1983, when Jannie's daughter Lisa was sixteen, she came to live with Jannie after living with Jannie's parents since she was born. Of course, Lisa had visited her mother regularly in the summers and during the Christmas holidays. But not until she was sixteen did Lisa agree to live with her Mom full time.

"It turned out that living with my parents was very good for Lisa," says Jannie. "My parents adored Lisa. They were very close. Lisa spoke at both of their funerals about her early childhood and how wonderful it was to have her grandparents' undivided attention. I think for them, it was almost like 'we've raised ten kids and now we have a grandkid we can just play with and adore'. Once I started earning money, I did send money for Lisa's support. She told me, Grandmama and Granddaddy would tell me all the time, 'Now your mother's taking care of you and you're living with us. When you are older you can go live with your mother if you want. We will be okay, but we're glad you're here now'. The outcome was pretty good."

Divorce

As Jannie continued having success selling real estate, she believed she had finally gotten on solid enough ground financially to divorce Jim. It was liberating for her, but the aftermath was difficult.

She recalls that she wrote a note to herself, as a woman who was divorced and with two children: "Fear and doubt awakened in me, again. Even though I was doing well with earnings, I had never fully managed my own finances. My mother had managed my teenage earnings from the work I did for the Hansford family, and Jim had given me an allowance from my earnings, much like my mom had done."

Jannie rented an apartment in the Bellevue area of Nashville, but apartment living was not like living in a single-family home. "It had wooden walkways and folks would come home all hours of the night; they worked all hours, all different shifts. There were mostly young people in the apartments. It wasn't a high quality of life for me. I couldn't sleep as I was accustomed to sleeping in a quiet house. So, I decided, as someone had said to me, that living well is the best revenge. I moved back to my single-family home.

"I focused on living well. A girl at work asked me, 'Who's going to bring you flowers now?' I said I am. She laughed. To paraphrase Shakespeare, will the flowers I give myself smell as sweet as ones from a partner? Yes. I found that they do. I enjoy flowers on my breakfast room table all year long. I discovered, as a saving tip, that carnations will last three to four weeks. I can get a bunch of carnations at Wal-Mart for about $4. Therefore, my average cost is about $1 per week. I also have some roses that bloom in my yard from May to about September. I bring a few roses in from my yard.

"Living well for me has always been a personal triumph, a celebration of a life I almost ended twice by my own hands. So, perhaps that's the number one reason that I'm grateful for an opportunity to live well, and hopefully I'll be able to give back to help someone else, if by no other way than saying yes, you can make it, too. Divorce takes a lot out of folks, and sometimes it forces us to ask the hard questions. We need to discover the answers and make them work for ourselves, no matter the challenge."

Each year, Jannie continued to have success in her "second job" as a Realtor helping sellers and buyers. She hadn't yet reached her goal of financial independence, but she was laying the groundwork and she was saving some of the money she earned in real estate. Her other job as a dental hygienist, though, was causing her health problems.

After thirteen years in the profession, she had developed carpal-tunnel syndrome and had to have surgery in 1993. A doctor advised her that if she went back to work as a dental hygienist, her hand would not hold up. So, she talked with the director of the health department, who told her to apply for the next job that came open in health promotion. She got the job.

"Interestingly enough, considering my history as a teen mom, I worked in Adolescent Pregnancy Prevention," says Jannie. "I also did some anti-smoking work and some work involving healthy eating and exercise. We did health promotion activities in the schools from time to time."

"I enjoyed my work in health promotion. However, I could see that many people were not emotionally able or ready to alter their health habits. Smoking cessation seemed the hardest hurdle for patients. One patient said each time he tried to stop smoking, he had nightmares and was only able to sleep a few hours each night," Jannie says.

Another College Degree and a New Job

Even as Jannie had been working two jobs for many years, she also had gone back to college. In 1993, she earned a master's degree in Public Administration from TSU. That resulted in a new opportunity at the health department. The director, a board-certified pediatrician, asked Jannie to be her executive assistant. She accepted that job and when the director left, Jannie assisted the next director of health. Over the years, she worked as the executive assistant to three different directors.

"This was truly a positive sign for us black southerners. The initial director of health in 1977 wanted to pay me less because I was black. And then, I ended up working in the director's office for seventeen years. I am grateful for that experience."

Because a college education was always emphasized by Jannie's mother, she was of course very happy when Jannie got her bachelor's degree on June 6, 1977, but she was doubly happy in 1993 when Jannie earned a master's degree. Even her father was moved by her accomplishment.

"My father was very pleased, smiling and happy, but he never got as excited about education as mother did. However, I think it finally hit him that these kids are doing alright. They don't want to be farmers, but they're doing alright anyway. I think my parents had separate dreams for us. Thankfully my mother carried that banner of 'they need to go to school'.

"One of the biggest arguments I ever heard from my parents was when I was about seven and my older sister, Lucille, wanted to go to college in 1957. My mother at the time was pregnant with my brother Cleo. She was in the kitchen making biscuits and telling my dad all the reasons why he needed to take my oldest sister to college. He said, 'Really what I need is some help on this farm. We ain't got no college money. We already got debts and bills'. She was saying, 'How will we ever get anything? How will they ever do better if we're going to make them stay here and farm?'

"Dad was very slow and deliberate in his speech, and Mother was a rapid speaker. She could get in a lot more words than Dad. So, they would argue, but they never hit each other. I never heard them curse each other. I think, in large part, they tried to keep a lot of their disagreements away from us, but when you have ten kids in a small house, there's always a child snooping around, listening.

"I remember Mom crying the day she was begging Dad to drive Lucille to college in Nashville and give her the $151.50 for first quarter tuition, fees, housing and food. I realized that if Mom had the money, she would just send Lucille to college. But she had to beg for something that should have been available. As a seven-year-old child, I wished for enough money to help my Mother and sister. My sister was trying to do the right thing with her life. She just wanted to go to college. Mother had hope and expectations. Mom told Lucille that if she got a chance to go to college, she would need to work and pay some college expenses as well as complete all assignments. If Lucille failed in college, my Mom knew Dad would not even drive the rest of us to Nashville.

"After a few days of intense conversations, Dad finally agreed to drive Lucille to Tennessee State University in Nashville. He gave her the $151.50 required for the first quarter for an in-state student; this was a public school in 1957. Lucille worked, studied, pledged AKA, and graduated in four years. Mom was a motivator; Lucille was obedient. She set the trajectory for the nine of us who were born after her. Lucille admits today that the college situation presented a lot of pressure for her as a 17 year old; she withstood the pressure and grew stronger. She showed us that we, too, could complete college."

In the early to mid-1990s, while still working two jobs – at the health department and in real estate – Jannie was thinking more about her future and specifically how to achieve her goal of becoming financially independent. She was confident real estate would provide the path, but not if she only worked as an agent helping people sell their home or buy a home. What she needed to do, she decided, was to personally invest in real estate. How she would do that came in a way that even surprised her.

Chapter 6

A Path to Wealth

One of the lessons Jannie learned about investing in real estate came early on in her career. She recalls her broker, Dick Winecoff, talking about it during one of the training sessions he conducted for real estate agents.

"He said, 'You agents can make a living selling real estate, but you can become wealthy by owning real estate.' That statement really made sense to me."

Her path to owning didn't begin simply by finding and buying a property and leasing it. Jannie noticed a sign posted at a busy intersection in Brentwood. A real estate agent, Susan Kelton, had placed the sign, which said: "I need houses to rent, good income."

Jannie contacted Susan, who came to take a look at Jannie's house, a three-bedroom, two-bath, one-story with a two-car garage in a nice subdivision with a Brentwood address at the edge of Davidson County, less than two miles from Interstate

65. Jannie liked her house, but she no longer needed that much space because her daughters had moved. She also reasoned that if she could rent the house, she could live nearby for a while with her older sister Rose.

"When Susan told me what my house would rent for, my jaw dropped. She said, 'About $1,800 per month. I have executives that are looking for property.' I was shocked. I said, 'How soon could you lease it?' 'Probably tomorrow,' she said. A light bulb popped on in my head. I thought, "Wow! This sounds like an easy way to make money!"

At that time, in the 1990s, Nissan Motor Corporation was bringing in executives from Japan because they were constructing a factory to build automobiles in Smyrna, just down the road from Brentwood.

Susan leased Jannie's house and Jannie moved in with Rose. "I thought it would be fun to live with Rose because we always got along so well together. I negotiated with her about what to pay, and I let her know I worked a lot. I said I can't do your cooking and cleaning, so you have to factor that in. We had a great time. I stayed with her a while and then I decided I would buy a condominium or a house."

New single-family homes were being built in the Nolensville Road area and in November 1995, Jannie purchased one for $126,000. Because she planned on living in it, her financing terms were much better than if she were buying it to lease to tenants. She only had to put down about 5 percent versus 20 percent if she were buying the house as an investment. She lived in the house for about six months and then decided to buy a condominium to live in. She leased the house. She is happy she kept it because in 2022, the house had an estimated value of $367,000. Plus, it has generated good rental income for more than 25 years.

Early on, Jannie says she was really taken by the idea of investing in a house to rent. "It really struck me that you can rent it out and somebody else will pay for it. That was the only investment that others would pay off for me. If I bought some stock, I paid the whole price myself and hoped it would go up. Some stock went up. Some did not."

When she purchased the house, Jannie used savings for the down payment – savings accrued from working at the health department and as a Realtor. She had formed a habit of saving money. That become an important part of her strategy to buy homes.

Saving Is a Habit

"Starting from zero, many people, including myself, have trouble saving that first down payment to buy that first house. It can become a major hurdle. I focused on saving small amounts at first. I knew that if I were ever going to be financially independent, I needed to start making success-oriented decisions intentionally. For me, that meant starting with an attainable goal and building on that goal."

She used myriad ways to save her first $100. "It sounds petty, but if you duplicate it ten times, you have $1,000 to use toward a down payment. An innovative builder in our area recently sold several developments by offering first time home buyers $1,000 total out-of-pocket money to close if they were going to live in the house. The builder/developer covered all the other costs. So, saving is key. I encouraged myself and I told my clients, don't assume you need a huge amount of money to buy your first home. Your credit history is more important."

Whether it was food, clothing, household items or services, Jannie was diligent in saving money.

"I cut out all the fluff from the grocery list and purchased real food such as fruit, oatmeal, potatoes, salad greens, chicken, eggs, peanut butter. I looked for dollar-stretching meals like casseroles, quick and easy to make, and yielded leftovers for a second meal. My favorite meal for that, then and now, is tuna casserole. My children loved it, then and now. The recipe is basically canned tuna, elbow macaroni, chopped onion, cheese, and cream of mushroom soup. Don't throw your leftovers away. I saved my leftovers for a hungry, busy day; I had many such days.

"I stopped eating out regularly in order to save money. I carried my lunch to work four days each week, and I started to combine errands and trips to conserve gas. I wore more wash-and-wear clothes to avoid expensive dry-cleaning bills.

"I cut back on gifts. At Christmas, when I was saving to buy my second rental property, I told my relatives I was saving to buy a house. They understood and they appreciated the small gifts I purchased. My siblings and I realized it was the fellowship we valued most – singing, laughing, playing games, rehashing family stories – not the gifts. Eventually we eliminated individual gift giving. For decades now, we have played a Dirty Santa game in lieu of individual gifts. We love it.

"It took me about three weeks before I had saved my first $100. I knew if I continued and looked for other opportunities to save, I could reach my goal. After about six months, I received a small raise at work. All of that $30 per month raise went directly to my savings account. My saving habit had taken root."

Jannie said she shined her own shoes and

washed her car. She also saved by doing her own hair and nails. For several consecutive years I skipped out-of-town vacations. I opted instead to do fun summer activities in Nashville with my children. I knew that by foregoing instant gratification, I could reach a time when tenants would be funding our vacations, spa appointments and car washes.

"I learned that saving routinely on small items can make a huge difference over time. Paper towels cost about $1.50 per roll. I once used one to two rolls of paper towels per week. Each time I rinsed my hands off while cooking or cleaning the kitchen, I used a paper towel. I curtailed my use of paper towels years ago by using a designated hand towel. Then, during CO-VID in early 2020, I realized paper towels were in short supply. I went to the store one day and they weren't there. Lucky for me I had used a designated towel for my hands for many years. I dry my hands on that cloth. I keep that cloth separate from the other cloths I use in the kitchen. Paper towels are still present in my kitchen, but I use few of them. If I spill something on the floor, I use a paper towel. I'm probably saving three dollars a week just on paper towels. Saving is a habit.

"During the 1990s when I was looking for savings, I found lots of possibilities. I got an energy audit that nudged me to unplug appliances that

I wasn't using and to turn out lights when I left a room. I encouraged myself by looking at what I had accumulated. This positive self-feedback helped me to be disciplined. The money I saved was used for down payments on real estate."

Jannie also ate breakfast and most meals at home. She could see how much money some of her relatives and friends were spending on such things as frequent coffee purchases at Starbucks. "That amount of money on a daily basis, over a year's time, could go a long way toward a down payment, and maybe if you find the right builder/developer, it could be the down payment required to buy that first property."

Jannie believes that many of her saving methods would work even in today's times when it has become more difficult to make a dollar stretch.

She learned of one unusual saving technique from a friend who was saving for her first down payment to buy a house. The friend asked her landlord when it was time to renew her lease if he would decrease the monthly rent by $10 because she was never late with the rent and she took good care of the property. It was during a soft rental market, and her landlord agreed. The woman put that $10 per month into her savings account.

Landlords will sometimes agree to lower rent because they don't have the expense of cleaning the property for a new tenant. Plus, it often takes time and money to get the property prepared for a new tenant and then find a suitable tenant. "Every dollar helps," Jannie says. "Many landlords would consider this, if approached by good tenants."

Moving Forward

Saving and working two jobs helped Jannie buy a condominium for $159,700 not long after she had purchased the house for $126,000 to live in. Her plan was to live in the condo permanently. It had three bedrooms upstairs, with two baths. There was a half-bath downstairs with the kitchen, living room, a fireplace, a patio and a two-car garage. She felt it was about the right amount of space for her, 1,750 square feet. When she purchased it, she had two houses – one she was living in and one she was renting to tenants.

The condo was under construction when Jannie signed a contract for it. The unexpected happened. "I will never forget how that condo increased in value during the 14 months it was under construction. That was a huge eureka moment for me! Put a to-be-built property under contract and while they're building it, it appreciates. How cool is that? You make money and you are not even paying on a mortgage yet."

Jannie paid $159,700 for the condo under

construction, but when she closed, it appraised for $164,500. "I made almost $5,000 in the fourteen months I was waiting. I was ecstatic." About fifteen months after she closed, the condo appraised for $175,000. "These numbers confirmed for me that I was on the right track."

Construction was delayed to the point that Jannie had to move from her house because she had already agreed to lease it for $1,200 a month. So, she put her furniture in storage and moved back in with Rose until the condo was ready.

Jannie had hired Susan to lease the house because Jannie was busy working two jobs. She also had come to the conclusion that having a third-party represent her to handle leasing and rent collections was valuable. It cost her about 10 percent of the rent each month, but she says, "It was well worth it. I didn't have to worry about it."

"I think when some tenants meet with the landlord, they feel like they can tell their sad story and the landlord will wait on the rent or accommodate them in other ways. It is better for me to have a rental agent manage tenants."

Although Jannie bought the condo to live in, many people buy condos as an investment. Whether buying as an investor or as a primary resident, there are some criteria to consider when buying a condo versus buying a single-family home. She says it's especially important to look at the financial statements of the condominium association or homeowner association (HOA) and see if a "reserve study" has been done.

"The study looks at each item for which the HOA is responsible (roof, siding, landscaping, etc.) and determines whether enough money will be in reserves to cover the cost when that item is worn out and needs to be replaced. Some items cost thousands of dollars such as replacing roofs on 150 condos, repaving the streets, replacing siding and renewing the landscaping just to name a few. Will the money be there? If HOAs do not have a reserve study, and they're not properly funding the amounts needed for maintenance, repairs, replacement, etc., there can be huge cash assessments due from each owner in years to come." Also, she adds, it's important to make sure an HOA is financially sound before submitting an offer.

It is best practice to review the covenants and restrictions for any property you are planning to buy (if any such documents exist). Condos and most subdivisions in Middle Tennessee have governing documents.

Although Jannie's investment portfolio at this time had only two single family homes she was leasing, she was fascinated by the amount of rent people were paying her and other investors like her.

So, she cut back on working with clients looking to buy or sell real estate and instead focused on building a portfolio of investment properties.

Jannie soon discovered a new source of homes for investments. The Veterans Administration – known formally as the U.S. Department of Veterans Affairs – was selling homes it had foreclosed on. The VA set the price, didn't negotiate and would not make any repairs, but it did provide financing. Jannie found a home north of Murfreesboro in Smyrna. It had three bedrooms, one-and-a-half baths, an eat-in kitchen and central heat and air. There was no garage, but it had a nice large level lot. The VA was the lender and processor and required only $500 down. Jannie bought the house for $89,000 and got a 7 percent VA loan.

The home needed some renovation, but Jannie's criteria for buying VA-foreclosed homes was to find those that didn't need substantial work. She wasn't the type of person who could do the construction or renovation, so she hired contractors while she worked to get the yard and outside of the house in shape. Even with the cost of renovation, Jannie knew the property could pay for itself and produce rental income for years if she kept it.

Once repairs were made, she leased the house – and it's never been vacant for long in the 24 years she has owned it. Today, its value is estimated at $272,000. Rental income is currently$1,225 a month – $14,700 per year.

She purchased another VA-foreclosed property, did some work on it and leased it for a year before selling it for a profit. "By selling it after a year, the profit became long-term capital gains rather than short-term. If I had just purchased it, rehabbed it and sold it, the profit would have been taxed as short-term gain. There are tax considerations to keep in mind with real estate and it's important to understand those and manage them. I took the advice of my tax expert. I do not offer tax advice; however, I believe real estate offers more tax shelter than almost any other investment. Talk with your tax expert."

Although "location, location, location" has to be top of mind when buying real estate, sometimes it's still viable to invest in a run-down neighborhood that's in a not-so-great location. In 1998, Jannie was asked by a fellow Realtor to look at one of his listings in a less-than-desirable neighborhood within walking distance of downtown Nashville. North Nashville at the time was inhabited by many low-income residents and the condition of the properties reflected the fact that people didn't have much money to spend on upkeep. Crime rates were high.

The 1,050 square-foot one-bath house, with central heat and air and three bedrooms, was being sold as-is, which meant it needed some work and the owner wasn't going to do any repairs. Jannie wasn't excited about investing in North Nashville at the time; however, she considered some advice she had received as a member of the Real Estate Investment Club of Nashville (REIN): "It really doesn't have to be a great neighborhood for you to make a great return. You just need to have a property that people will rent."

Jannie thought the area would eventually go up. And, one of her friends who was an appraiser, said at the time that North Nashville would one day be a very desirable place to live, and property will be valuable because it's the only part of Nashville from which a person can walk to downtown. "That's exactly what has happened," Jannie says. "It has taken years, but now 37208 is one of the hottest zip codes in Nashville and Middle Tennessee."

In 1998 Jannie purchased the North Nashville house for $40,000, renovated it and leased it to Section 8 tenants. "The young people who live there now love it. The tenants are young, urban professionals." It's always been easy to rent. Today, Jannie says the value of the house is about $310,000.

In 2004, Jannie purchased another home in North Nashville for $41,000. Today, its estimated value is $323,000. It, too, has been easy to keep rented – current rent is $1,100 a month – but she says the house is more than 70 years old and has some issues that may cause her to tear it down and build two structures on the lot because Metro Codes Department will allow it. The lot is valuable because the neighborhood is undergoing regentrification. When she bought the house, it was a Fannie Mae foreclosure, but unlike the V A foreclosures, she had to get conventional financing to buy the house. Because it was a Fannie Mae foreclosure, she was only required to put five percent down.

Section 8 Rentals

Jannie did try to sell the older house a year or so after she purchased it, but she got no offers, so she continued to lease it. She leased it to a tenant as part of the Section 8 federal housing program in which the government helps low-income earners pay their rent. Some investors dislike leasing their homes in the Section 8 program because of extra paperwork, regulations and rules that require owners to make repairs even though the tenants caused the damage.

A Look at the Numbers:
Return on Investment

In 1985 Jannie purchased a home for her primary residence. After living in it for eight years, she leased it. In 2022 she still owned the house.

The 1985 purchase price was $145,000; it offered three bedrooms, two baths and a two-car garage.

"My 10 percent down payment was $14,500 and closing costs were about 4 percent, $5,800. So, my total out-of-pocket cost was $20,300. The house today is valued at about $540,000. Rental income since I began renting it out averages about $21,000 a year. (Current monthly rent is $2,200 or $26,400 per year.)"

When she leased it to tenants starting in 1993, she still owed about $130,000 on the mortgage. In approximately seven years the tenants paid the mortgage in full. Since the tenants paid off the mortgage in 2000, the cash flow has averaged approximately $21,000 per year for 22 years. This created a gross cash flow of approximately $462,000. The cash flow plus the increased value of $540,000 contributed about one million dollars to Jannie's quest for financial independence.

"Once the property is paid off, the income is there to use indefinitely. The cash-on-cash return over time is a wealth-builder because the investor has the advantage of the equity build-up and the cash flow."

As part of her investment strategy, did she consider selling the property at any time over the years? There really wasn't a good reason to sell it, she says. She would have had to consider the cost to replace it and the income she could get from the new property.

"Tax considerations are important," she says. An investor and instructor at REIN told her that "once all the depreciation was gone, he would fix up the property and sell it." Jannie uses a straight line 30-year depreciation, which gives a lot of time before the depreciation is gone. Investors who hold on to the property can refinance it and take cash out. Re-fi money is not taxable. Real estate serves as a great big piggy bank if an investor wants to use it that way. So, the incentives for selling a property are not that great because even if you need cash, you can pull it out," Jannie says.

A second example of a healthy return is the Nolensville Road area house Jannie purchased for her primary residence in 1995 for $126,000. Her total out-of-pocket costs were $11,300 ($6,300 or 5% for the down payment and about $5,000 or 4 percent for closing costs). Today, the home is valued at $367,000.

In seven years, from 1996 to 2003, the rental income from the tenants paid the mortgage in full. "Since 2003, the cash flow has been approximately $18,000 per year for 19 years or $342,000. The cash flow of $342,000 plus the increased value of $367,000 combined to improve Jannie's financial foundation by $709,000."

A third example is the house Jannie purchased in 1998 for $40,000 in North Nashville, within walking distance of downtown. She bought the house, as an investor, with no intention of living in it. So, her down payment was 20 percent, or $8,000. The seller, who was anxious to sell, paid Jannie's closing costs.

"The house is currently valued at $308,500," Jannie says. "It has been leased from 1998 to 2022, or 24 years. The rental income has averaged $1,000 per month. The tenants paid off the $32,000 mortgage debt in approximately four years. Since 2002, the cash flow has been approximately $12,000 per year, times the 20 years, or $240,000. The home is currently rented for $1,100 per month. It could rent for more, but the tenants are good, so I'm not rocking the boat with them."

"If I total the market value of $308,000 with the cash flow of $240,000 since the house was paid off in 2002, that equals a total of $548,000. An investment of $8,000 in 1998 has improved my current net worth by $548,000. It's a robust return."

Jannie says, "In real estate investing there are triple forces: the forces of leverage, which is the use of other people's money; appreciation or increasing values which include compounding; and the force of cash flowing in the first of every month. All of these forces combine to make real estate a golden investment."

The examples above show what is possible by investing in real estate. "Admittedly, Nashville's real estate market has been extraordinary during the past decade. However, robust returns are possible across the nation."

Investing in real estate is cited in *Money 101*, a book written in 2008 by Jannie's niece, Pamela Pitts. "You make money when the value of the property increases. If you own rental property, you also get income from the property," Pamela writes.

She also mentions compounding, which pays big dividends for investors. "If you invested a lump sum of $10,000 for 10 years at 8 percent rate of return you would accumulate $21,589.25. If you invested the same amount at the same rate of return but instead invested it for 20 years you would accumulate $48,609.57! But remember, the money can't grow if you withdraw it. Think of your investment as a tree, a money tree that you want to grow. The longer you allow your money tree to grow the bigger it will be!"

Jannie's investments have shown how the principle also applies to real estate. She has earned hundreds of thousands of dollars by holding onto many of her properties over the years.

In the early 2000s, Jannie was by then quite

comfortable with owning and managing investment properties. Rental property provided "passive income," which Pamela wrote about in *Money 101*: "How much passive income do you need? The simple answer is that you want enough passive income every year to cover the cost of things you need and the things you want. You want to be able to live off of the income from your investments. Think of your investments as a goose. The passive income would then be all of the eggs laid by the goose. Remember, you can never eat the goose, only the eggs."

Jannie was doing well with her investments – and still working at the health department and as a Realtor. But in the early 2000s, a potential partner approached her about working together to buy houses to renovate and sell. Jannie hadn't been thinking about having a partner – and she wasn't sure she needed one.

Chapter 7

Renovating for a Quick Profit

A long-time health department employee where Jannie worked asked Jannie about becoming investment partners. Jannie's response: "Really, I just try to keep the health department separate from my real estate life as much as I can. The person replied, 'Well I know you've helped some people buy property because I've heard them talking about it in the breakroom. So, we could partner, and I won't even talk about it.'

The potential partner wasn't a Realtor, but like Jannie, she was a member of REIN and she was anxious to begin investing. "She was intelligent, but she doubted herself a lot. She told me this was something she always wanted to do. When she was a child, around nine years old, her family was evicted right at Christmas, it was snowing, and she shared some memories with me of her mother holding her and the two of them crying because they had to move. She didn't understand why they had to leave their home. When she shared this childhood story with me, it summoned memories of my childhood and I thought, she's a kind person, so let's give it a try."

Many of the real estate issues the partners dealt with were the same as if they had been working separately: Finding houses to purchase at the right price; determining the number of homes to buy; where to buy; securing a line of credit from the bank; finding and working with contractors during renovation; determining the costs and types of renovation needed and a timeline for completing and selling the property; and the effects of the economy in recessionary or inflationary times.

"As partners we agreed to only hold jointly held property long enough to rehab and sell it. Each of us could still buy properties to keep in our own name. We decided the ownership was clearer and the tax situation was clearer if we just purchased together and then when we sold it, we would split the profit and expenses," Jannie says. "We each claimed that on our taxes, and we were done until we found another property. We both agreed that we wouldn't involve others in what we were doing, and we didn't because we knew how that could complicate things."

Jannie's partner was analytical and she learned to estimate what it was going to cost to renovate a property. "She was a hands-on person"

Jannie says. "When a toilet was running she would retool it and it would work. We were a good team." Jannie realized quickly that the partnership offered added financial resources, a second set of hands for getting things done, an additional brain for stronger decisions and a comrade.

Jannie spent a lot of time finding potential homes to buy, arranging appointments to view them, and eventually, marketing the property they purchased. Her partner worked closely with the contractors, making sure they were doing what was needed.

As members of REIN, Jannie and her partner received a lot of advice and had access to many resources. One of the first and most important steps they learned was to review their credit report, clean it up if necessary and then establish a relationship with a bank so they would have a line of credit available when they were ready to make a purchase. Also, they were advised to get a letter showing they were pre-approved for a loan because that strengthened any offer they made.

"REIN instructors said credit was our greatest asset," Jannie recalls. "They advised us to borrow from a small community bank rather than a large one. The small banks were subjected to the Community Reinvestment Act, which requires lenders to participate in loans for certain geographical areas. REIN also advised us that some of the smaller banks had more discretion in making loans because they had more decentralized underwriting."

An investor/instructor at REIN told them a proven approach to improve their chances of obtaining a loan from a banker was to have their financial statements, three years of tax returns, and a resume in a binder. Other suggestions: Have a cover sheet indicating the personal financial statement was prepared for that specific bank. In the package, they should include their resumes and business experience. It's important for the banker to understand they were solid individuals. Include a list of memberships in organizations and clubs as well as personal references and business references. List education credentials. Include a credit report. List assets. Present all the information in a neat, professional portfolio.

"I remember that after I followed these guidelines, it gave me confidence to walk into the bank and present myself for a loan," Jannie says.

Jannie and her partner were well-received when they first went to meet a banker who reviewed their portfolio and documents. He immediately considered them serious investors rather than partners who hadn't prepared. The banker set them up with a line of credit and provided a letter that showed they were pre-approved for a loan. They continued to use that bank for most of their purchases.

Jannie recalls a disturbing experience at one bank – the one where she also had her personal account in the late 1990s or early 2000s. She felt as if she was re-living the past. Because of racism, she says, she was initially denied a good interest rate. She had wanted to refinance the mortgage for the house she was living in and she knew the rates other REIN members were receiving.

"The African American woman who was my loan officer offered me a rate that was higher than what my colleagues were getting to refinance. I said to her, 'Why am I getting this rate?' She said, 'That's what my supervisor said we could do.' We talked a little bit and I said this is racism. I said some of the investors in REIN are full-time investors; that's all they do. My loan is a lot safer because I have an income, a stable job (at the health department), plus I sell real estate. And I have good credit. So, this is what you're going to offer me? She said, 'This is just what I can do.' I said, here's what we're going to do. You tell your supervisor if I don't get a better rate, then I'm going to go to The Tennessean newspaper, and I think I can make this a very interesting story.

"The loan officer came back the next day with an interest rate of what it should have been. I wondered how many black people were being treated this way? My personal case proved to me that black people are charged extra interest because we are black – not because of a bad credit rating."

The small community bank used by investors, Jannie says, seemed fairer than the large bank that offered a higher than market rate for Jannie's primary residence. For the partnership, they were able to primarily use their line of credit at the community bank to buy a house and renovate it rather than having to put up personal funds.

"The banks would normally let us borrow up to 80 percent of the after-repair value of the property," Jannie says. "When we went to the bank, they would say here's your pre-approval letter. When you find a property, send or bring us the contract. Then, the bank called its appraiser to do an after-repair appraisal. If the appraiser said, after it's repaired, this house will be worth $100,000, then we could borrow up to $80,000. So, the purchase price could include closing costs and the rest of the money we could get as a draw, as we had repairs made.

"The banker reserved the right to go back and make sure those repairs were completed before they released the draw, but they rarely did that. They might have done that on the first property we purchased, but once they understood that we were serious investors, they didn't put much time into checking to make sure that we put a roof on, painted the house, etc. We used borrowed funds a lot.

The only time we would use our own money was if we had exhausted those funds. That rarely happened because we had a cushion in there that was supposed to be our profit. We wanted to estimate these as best we could."

One of the pair's first purchases was a smelly trashy house with tall weeds and broken-down furniture inside. "My partner and I cleaned out the house, swept the floors, cut the grass and nailed the mailbox back on the wooden post. The next day as we were finishing up a man drove by and asked if he could walk through the house. He offered us $5,000 more than we paid. We were very happy! Never underestimate the value of de-junking and cleaning a property. When we closed the transaction about a week later, the bank got their money back and we split our quick profit. The banker told us he now viewed us as seasoned investors."

Finding Properties

As a Realtor, Jannie had access to the Multiple Listing Service that featured properties for sale. Any beginning investor who is not a Realtor should seek out a Realtor to help them find their first property, Jannie says. Realtors are governed by a Code of Ethics and are usually knowledgeable, friendly and helpful. "Tap into this great community resource," she says.

In addition to MLS, the partners relied on other sources and methods, including some suggested by REIN. "They taught us how to look for properties everywhere: for-sale-by-owner signs and for-rent-by-owner signs. A lot of owners who are trying to manage their own property really don't enjoy it, and if you offer a decent price, they might sell you the house rather than keep dealing with tenants. There was also DFD, which meant Driving-For-Dollars. You drive through a neighborhood, and if a house looks empty and deserted and the grass is real tall, then you look into the tax records and send a letter to the owner. The owner may live out of town or they no longer need the property. They might agree to sell it. There was a saying: 'If the grass is tall, the price is small.'

"We were also told to check courthouse records, eviction warrants, and the probate docket, as well as contact survivors of the deceased who owned properties. A lot of times they don't want the property, they just want to sell it. Obituaries might guide us to properties that will go up for sale within the upcoming twelve months."

In newspapers and business journals, the pair also found notices of homes in pre-foreclosure or foreclosure.

Another source was to look for houses that had burned. "Sometimes, people are totally disgusted with the burned property and they will sell."

It's also possible to buy delinquent notes from lenders, and then foreclose on people. "I never bought a delinquent note from a lender, but I may try that in the future because houses are harder to find in Middle Tennessee. There are so many people looking for property in this area. It's very hard to find something and if you do, it's expensive," Jannie says.

Currently, many savvy investors are buying property through wholesalers. Wholesalers are people who find buyers for owners who want to sell. They may charge the buyer a finder's fee. Active wholesalers are in constant contact with many owners and investors. They may have the right property for you.

Tax sales, where properties are being auctioned on the courthouse steps because owners didn't pay their taxes, are another place to acquire property. Different localities have different rules and regulations on how they advertise and handle tax sale property. So, Jannie advises investors to understand the rules in their county.

Some counties auction their tax delinquent properties two times a year. The successful bidder can sometimes get a nice property at a good price. There is a caveat to buying at tax sales, though. Usually, the owner of record has the legal right to redeem the property in a specified amount of time after the tax sale. In Nashville, she says, it is usually one year. If the previous owner pays their back-taxes and redeems the property, the person who bought the property at the auction will get their money back with interest at whatever the rates are at that time, she says.

"We were advised to board up the property for a year," Jannie says. "That's the safe thing to do if you're fortunate enough to get something at a tax sale. You board it up until you're certain that it's yours. Another glitch in buying tax sale property is that the title search sometimes gets fuzzy. So, title insurance companies are not eager to issue title insurance on tax sale property. That's another thing to keep in mind. A title company may opt to wait three years before issuing title insurance."

There also are many properties that banks take back because people haven't paid their mortgages. Some of the big banks will put several properties in one package and sell them to large investors. Some, though, have individual properties listed and people can buy a single home or condo that the bank owns.

Auctions also can be a good place to buy property. "Sometimes on bad weather days people don't show up much, so if it's cold and snowing, it's a good day to go to an auction," Jannie says.

REIN stressed searching for absentee owners. Send letters to owners whose mailing address is different than the property address and they may be more open to selling. Also, the city and county departments that issue code violations often have a list of condemned properties; these can be another source of possible houses to purchase.

Where to buy, which areas of town or which neighborhoods are decisions investors must make. While having "geographic diversity" – buying property in different sections of a city or even different cities – may have advantages, Jannie suggests investors buy where they can afford to buy.

"When you're looking for a property, you're looking for something you can make a profit on, or you're looking for something that you can rent-out long term. It has to be affordable, number one. Affordability is always a big factor."

Sometimes homes in a nearby city may be more affordable. The outlook for appreciation in home values, growth and demand for homes is positive. Those are reasons many people invest in properties a few hours from where they live. Most of the required time, effort and travel are in the early stages of the process: finding a property, having inspections done, completing the purchase and overseeing contractors doing the renovation. After the property is leased through a management company, investors don't have to make trips to the property. Pictures are often emailed or texted to property owners to keep them informed.

During the time of Jannie's partnership – in the early 2000s – they looked for houses that were under $100,000 so they could renovate them and list them for sale at about $150,000, which they felt was an affordable price range for many homebuyers.

"Each investor has to find their comfort level as to the price of homes they want to purchase. There are investors who don't want to be bothered if the house won't sell for half-a-million dollars when it's renovated because they don't believe there is enough profit to tie up their working capital and time," Jannie says. "Some REIN members didn't want to do any deals if they couldn't make $20,000. Sometimes they would call us because if we could make even $10,000 and split it, that was fine with us. During our first year of rehabbing, if we could make $5,000 each, we would rehab."

Before purchasing a house to renovate, Jannie advises investors to have a good understanding of the types of repairs that will be needed and how much they will cost. "REIN also stressed making sure the kitchens and baths were in good shape because they help sell the property. Also, install central heat and air if the house doesn't have it. Know that the steeper the roof line, the more expensive it will be to replace it. Also, don't forget about the outside of the house. Curb appeal sells property."

Investors, of course, always have to evaluate their property purchases in the context of economic conditions such as a recession or when inflation is high and interest rates are rising. Consider not just rates for loans or lines of credit, but also the mortgage rates buyers will likely pay to purchase the renovated house.

An instructor at REIN, Hal Wilson, who owned hundreds of rentals, told investors his favorite rental property to own during a recession was a five-room house, about 800 square feet, because it's essentially the least expensive and smallest place a family is likely to want: Living room, kitchen, two bedrooms and a bathroom. Jannie recalls Hal saying, "You'll go through some recessions and just remember, the smallest houses will be the easiest to keep rented."

"Hal was right," she says. "In 2008, those small single-family homes were the ones people were trying to get. They would say, 'let me get a small house, the least amount of rent and see if I can make it until this recession blows over and I can find a better job.'"

While there is no specific ideal number of homes an investor should buy and rehab each year – it depends on each investor – Jannie and her partner tried to purchase, renovate and sell about four houses a year. That number will vary for each investor based on his or her resources (including amount of time available) and comfort level. Some investors rehab one property each year.

The minimum amount the pair wanted to clear on each home they purchased was $5,000 each. "That doesn't sound like much, but for us at that time, it was an acceptable amount," Jannie says. "So, we had that minimum in mind when we did our calculations for what it would take to buy, rehab, and sell a house. We cleared more than that on all the properties except on one house we purchased that was in a flood plain. Flood insurance was required, and we barely broke even on that one. We had it under contract for a great price, but when the couple found out they had to pay for flood insurance and how much that would cost, they were afraid the house would flood. So, they walked away from the deal. Then we ended up selling it just to get out of it. Everything else we worked on together, we made more than $5,000 each."

Partnerships: Advantages and Disadvantages

For some people, having a partner is ideal. For others, working alone is the only way to go. Like most things in life, a partnership comes with pros and cons.

"I will say the pros outweigh the cons. My partners provided added financial inputs and valuable advice. Partners also helped me find suitable properties.

The downside is the risk that the partner may not be trustworthy. If the partner runs into legal problems of any type, the property may be slapped with a lien.

"In our partnership, we were both in agreement when we purchased a property. The hardest part for my partner was signing the first contract. She was hesitant. But after the first one, when she saw how it worked and we made a profit, she became more comfortable. The first transaction scares people the most."

"For each of us, it was a successful business partnership."

As an investor, Jannie also entered a partnership in 2013 to build two residences on a single vacant lot and then sell the homes. This was different than her experience of buying existing homes and either keeping them to lease to tenants or to renovate and sell.

"I told him I would partner with him if we could agree on the builder and the interior designer so that once it was finished, it would be something people would really want and not just something that we built out of our ideas."

The dwelling, called a horizontal property regime because each buyer owns their side, was similar to a duplex. Each side had 1,890 square feet. The first floor offered a great room with fireplace, kitchen with granite, stainless steel appliances dining area, powder room, a flex room and hardwood floors throughout. Upstairs there were two large bedrooms with baths and walk in closets attached. Each home had three outdoor living spaces, climate-controlled storage and was within walking distance of downtown Nashville.

"I really loved the final look of these homes and almost purchased one to live in myself," Jannie says. "It was the most expensive project I've partnered on to date. We spent about $365,000 to build the two. We sold one of them for $345,000 and the other one with the view of downtown for $355,000. We made a nice profit. It took about eight months to build and sell.

"Construction is another option for the real estate investor to consider. For me, it was an interesting and gratifying experience. I want to do more new construction."

Summary of Key Strategies

1. Work diligently to form positive habits – whether it's the habit of saving or enjoying regular physical activity. Form positive hab-

its. Positive habits lead to positive behavior.

2. If starting from zero dollars, set a small attainable savings goal – $100, $200 or $500. After you reach the first goal, your confidence in your ability to save will increase. The second goal will be easier. Try it – it works!

3. Tell family and close friends you are saving and investing for your future.

4. Tell everyone you know you are looking for real estate to purchase.

5. Work hard to buy your first property. Your property will work hard for you.

6. Conquer the fear of making the first purchase.

7. Buy early in your life and buy as often as possible.

8. Consult a Realtor. Realtors save you time and money. Realtors represent you through the entire transaction.

9. Cultivate a relationship with a community banker. Present yourself to the banker neatly dressed and with a binder containing your resume, financial statement, and income tax returns for the past three years. Explain that you want to be prequalified in order to invest in real estate.

10. After buying and living in your first property for a couple of years, consider buying your second property.

11. After living in your home for two years, check to see if refinancing could lower your monthly payment. Also, if you are paying a mortgage insurance premium (MIP), ask the lender about requirements for dropping the MIP.

12. Don't be afraid to move to another proper-

ty. Moving can make you money. Many wise Americans move every two or three years.

13. Before you move to another property, ask yourself if you can lease the current home and keep it in your portfolio.

14. If selling your personal residence or a re-habbed property, remember that curb appeal sells property. Spruce up the yard and exterior of the property.

15. Think long term. What will a single-family home in your area be worth 20 years from today?

Jannie's first renovated property completed in March 2001 was located at 6106 Pennsylvania Avenue, Nashville, Tennessee. Two new single-family homes are now on this lot.

Chapter 8

Success Principles and Best Business Practices

Over the years, Jannie purchased several properties to live in before turning them into rentals rather than selling them. That has been one of her keys to reaching financial independence. Today, she owns 12 properties she leases. Those include nine single family homes and three condominiums. The total value of the properties is about $4 million.

As a real estate investor for nearly 25 years, coupled with her work as a Realtor even before she began investing, Jannie has put into place, or learned from others, many "best-business practices" that form the foundation of how she works and shows why she has been successful. It's not just practical applications such as understanding the fundamentals of real estate or developing specialized business skills. It's also attitude, whether that means toward herself or others. It's about business and life.

Business Philosophy

"I approach business as an opportunity and a challenge. My basic premise is that I want to treat people the way I would want them to treat me. It helps make my decisions easier, whether it's in my work as an investor or real estate agent."

"For example, a lot of real estate agents say, 'I should tell my clients this or that, but I don't know whether they'll walk away.' My question is would you want them to tell you if they were in your situation? Sometimes they'll say, 'I reckon,' and I say, well I reckon we ought to tell them. Do the right thing. Let people know, and then they can decide. It is an opportunity and a privilege to serve others during business transactions. And, it's a challenge. Treat people the way you want to be treated. It's easier that way. You might not make as much money, but what you make you'll make with a clear conscience and you will enjoy it more. I value the relaxed feeling of a clear conscience."

Keys to Success

"The experience of hard work, the willingness to work hard, to miss some parties, to miss some vacations, to delay gratification, and to focus are some of the keys to success."

A Good Deal

"Some say a business deal is not a good deal unless it's a good deal for both sides. It should not be that you really won and the other person lost. There is such a thing as a win-win."

Habits for Success

"Hard work, saving, saying thank you and please, and treating people the way I want to be treated."

Persistence

"Some great philosopher once said 'it's the struggle that keeps us strong'."

A Maxim for Life and Living

"Life is business, and business is life. Learn one, and you will have also learned the other." *Thou Shalt Prosper: Ten Commandments for Making Money* by Rabbi Daniel Lapin.

"Exercise the mind and the body every day."

"Apply yourself to thinking through difficulties – hard times can be softened, tight squeezes widened, and heavy loads made lighter for those who can apply the right pressure." *On Tranquility of Mind* by Seneca; *The Daily Stoic* by Ryan Holiday and Stephen Hanselman.

Adapt

"I learned from biology that living creatures that survive over time are those able or willing to adapt to the change in the environment. Adaptation is an essential skill. When my bosses changed, I altered actions to align with their methods of work. Change is a part of life. Even though I do not look forward to change, I know it is inevitable. Therefore, I must adapt. In real estate sales, it is essential to adapt to each client's needs and wants. As a real estate investor, it's also essential to adapt to each situation."

"And this in turn presupposes the human capacity to creatively turn life's negative aspects into something positive or constructive. In other words, what matters is to make the best of any given situation." *Man's Search For Meaning* by Viktor E. Frankl.

Attitude

"I like the saying that 'attitude determines your altitude'. The executive who introduced me to public health administration, Fredia Stovall Wadley, M.D., gave me valuable advice. During the interview, I told her I knew very little about public health administration. I only knew dental hygiene and how we operated the dental clinic. She said, 'I can teach you about public health. What I can't teach you is attitude. If you maintain a positive attitude, listen, and avail yourself of reading materials that I'll point out to you, you'll have a rewarding career in public health.' Dr. Wadley said attitude is the key, the vital component we cannot teach.

"That early advice made me keenly aware of my attitude. I took an attitude-mometer during my first year as Dr. Wadley's assistant. My aim was to be positive, friendly and pleasant in all situations. That was a challenge. Looking back years later, I'm convinced that attitude matters. I carried that out the door with me every day working in real estate. It was very helpful."

Character

"It means doing the right thing because it is the right thing to do, and not because I'll go to hell or I might get caught. I have to live with myself. I am reminded of a poem by Edgar Albert Guest, who said, 'I have to live with myself and so I want to be fit for myself to know'. Positive character equals a clear conscience and a good night's sleep. I like to sleep at night."

Ethics

"Ethics is doing things the right way from the beginning to end."

Consultants

"Consultants add value. Once I was rehabbing a rather large house, but it had a very small, old kitchen space. My business partner said just leave it small. I knew a small kitchen equaled a smaller selling price than what we needed for this size house. I consulted with the contractor and interior designer. The contractor, after scratching his head and pacing in the kitchen, found a space adjoining the kitchen that was underneath the stairs leading to the second floor. The interior designer and the contractor used that space as a walk-in pantry and shifted the refrigerator across from the pantry, erected a half wall between the kitchen and dining room, and magically the kitchen looked large. It was larger. Women select more houses than men, therefore baths and kitchens sell houses. Consultants have saved me money and are well-worth the time and effort they add to the value of the property."

Creative Thinking

"Creative thinking flows better for me in the mornings when I'm rested and my brain is uncluttered. My subconscious mind seems to work as a mobile phone that connects me to the Creator. Answers to problems and challenges often flow to me in the mornings. Answers to what seemed to be insurmountable challenges yesterday creep into my mind upon awakening. That is what I think of as divine intervention."

Decision-Making

"Decision-making is a process. I try to research to avail myself of information related to the decision. I make a list of pros and cons, and I ask myself what is the worst that can happen. I remind myself of one thing that I learned in grad school: to do nothing is an option and that is a decision. I often check in with an appropriate consultant, trusted friend, or family member as part of the process of making tough decisions."

Determination

"For me, determination is the clawing, clinging desire to continue, to know I cannot quit. That feeling sometimes propelled me forward. One example is early in my first year of dental hygiene studies. It occurred to me that I was not as prepared as several of the other students. Three classmates already had a Bachelor of Science degree. I felt dumb and thought about leaving school. Then reality hit. If I left, I would owe the money I had borrowed for that year. Plus, I would go back to a clerk's salary for the rest of my life. I didn't want to do that. I didn't want to step back. I focused, asked for extra help from instructors, and thankfully that help was provided.

I hung on until the subject matter started to make sense, and I never looked back after that. The beginning was tough, and it was sheer determination that kept me in the game."

Follow-up

"I made a note to myself to return clients' calls the same day, even on very long days. I tried to do what I promised I would do."

Gratitude

"Gratitude has helped me tremendously. I begin each day with thanks. I read many years ago that some great thinker once said, "Gratitude and depression cannot exist in the mind at the same time." I started putting more conscious mind-time into being grateful, concentrating on what I had, rather than what I didn't have. I started to think about things that went right for me, rather than those that went wrong. I became grateful for folks who helped me, rather than harboring resentment towards those who slighted me. Gratitude requires conscious effort and focus. It's the way I start my day. Gratitude pairs perfectly with my first cup of coffee."

Physical Work, Mental Work

"Hard work builds physical muscle. Mentally hard work strengthens the mind. Both breed success. I like this quote from Herophilus (325 B.C.), who was the physician to Alexander the Great: 'When health is absent, wisdom cannot reveal itself, art cannot become manifest, strength cannot fight, wealth becomes useless, and intelligence cannot be applied.'"

Integrity
"To me, integrity means who am I when no one is looking? I really like what Warren Buffet said about integrity. His father told him integrity was like virginity. It could be preserved but never restored. I think that's profound. That says it all about integrity."

Managing Myself
"I think of myself as running a small business. Each day, I consider what is the most important thing I need to accomplish or do for my business today. I am the Chief Executive Officer, the Chief Operating Officer, the Chief Financial Officer of me, and that is a big responsibility. So, I need to use my time wisely."

"In learning to manage myself, I was able to reconnect with my earlier goals of helping my parents, not living the rest of my life in poverty and being able to send my children to college. All of those goals helped me to focus and created some willingness to say it's alright to miss two or three parties. If I don't go on vacation this year, I know why. The self-management was partly a trade-off. I realized I couldn't have everything, but I could accomplish some things. Finally, my brain developed enough to analyze choices and make better selections."

Self-Confidence

"Small, successful endeavors helped me build self-confidence. Improved self-confidence enabled me to take larger steps. So, I found that just being successful at small things did wonders in terms of making me feel like I could do it."

Self-Evaluation

"After each transaction, I made notes, mental and written, about what went well, what went wrong, and what I should look out for or improve the next time. I tried to be honest with myself. This self-assessment helped me avoid similar mistakes the next time around. I have advised my children to not be afraid to self-evaluate. You don't need to beat yourself up, but you do need to be honest."

Lessons from Teachers

"One day a professor told me that the human brain is not fully developed until age twenty-five. I then realized what had happened to me. My brain was not fully developed when I made some major life decisions that included becoming pregnant at sixteen, marrying and becoming a college dropout at nineteen."

"Another teacher that I remember gave me a pep talk on race. He was a psychology professor and he said to me, 'You have as much right to be here as anybody else, so concentrate on the class and what you're learning and not on your classmates. Participate and get as much out of this as you can. Don't overanalyze it'.

"Another professor said to essentially use your own brain. Think, don't be afraid to think and reason for yourself. Once you do that, you will realize that your thoughts will lead you in the right direction. My most difficult task was learning to manage myself because at one point I would make decisions that were self-destructive, not in my best interest. I would just go along with whatever, and really didn't engage my brain to think about what that meant for me. I was at least twenty-one before I had a clue about self-management. Then I fully connected my poor decisions to my life situation. That helped me to take responsibility for the decisions I had made in the past.

"Once I understood that my brain wasn't fully mature or developed when I made some life changing decisions, it helped me forgive myself, to say you weren't quite there yet, but now you are. So, you can use that experience and the lessons you've learned, and with a mature brain you should be able to make better decisions. That was helpful in managing myself going forward."

Lessons from Parents

"Don't be afraid of hard work. Put music, laughter and joy into your work. Work ain't never killed nobody. Love and get along with your siblings. Obey those in authority. Love your neighbor. Worship God. Remember the Sabbath and keep it Holy. Waste not, want not. If you stumble or fall, get up and dust yourself off."

Measuring Success

"Money does not equate to success. Success for me is peace with my soul. Yes, money is necessary. It can buy comfortable things and give us options, but money alone cannot make you feel good about yourself. Money won't guarantee you a good night's sleep or friends to give you honest feedback and emotional support. Money can't wish me a happy birthday or sit with me when I'm recovering from illness. Money can't say 'I love you, I appreciate you, you are important to me'. Money is a thing, an object. Success is far more important than money. Success is inner peace and a heart filled with love."

Organization

"Over the years, I developed a method of organizing things so I can get to them efficiently. I learned to do part of this when I was working as an assistant to three different directors of health. In business, being organized has saved me a lot of time. I could quickly pull out the information I needed. If an agent said, you all didn't ask us to leave the refrigerator, I could say 'here it is on page two of the contract'. So, it helped in that way."

"In my home life, now in semi-retirement, one example of organization is cards of various kinds. I like to send sympathy cards, get-well cards, birthday cards to people, as well as graduation cards and anniversary cards to some dear friends. I was forever looking for cards that I had purchased. I couldn't find them, so I devised a way of using brown paper bags, sticking all birthday cards in one bag, all get-well cards in another, etc. I wrote at the top of the bag what cards were contained inside. I put them in a plastic file box, and now I never look for cards again. I also know when my supply is getting low, and I can go to the store and restock. That's just an

From Poverty to Prosperity

example of organization that has helped."

Recessions

"I think of recessions as a cooling of the economy, a time to catch my breath and look for good deals and make plans for the recovery. It isn't necessarily a time to withdraw. Recessions are part of the natural cycle, and they're necessary so the economic engine won't overheat."

Strengths

"I believe one of my strengths is that I genuinely like most people. The clients that I met over the years seem like friends. I'm not in contact with all of them all the time, but when I bump into them, it feels like I'm talking with an old friend.

"I'm really somewhat of an introverted person yet I'm able to connect with people on a human real-life level. Clients felt comfortable with me, and I felt comfortable with them."

Weaknesses

"I am an impatient person. I am opinionated. Sometimes I am judgmental. Constantly I work to improve."

Work-Life Balance

"I made a list of the things that I enjoy. I try to find time to do things I enjoy. For most of the years, work-life balance skewed toward working too much. I did make some conscious decisions to work, and real estate is an interesting business. Once you start working with a client, how do you tell them 'it's taking you too long, I'm going to let you go, I don't want to be bothered with you, you're too picky?' What we tend to do is put in more hours and try to solve the riddle. What is the right place for this person at this time in their life, with the money that they're able to invest? Sometimes in order to answer those questions, it requires even starting 20 miles or more outside the city and looking for homes in a different community. It can involve a lot of time."

Purpose of Business

"Of course, it was to help myself, but it was also to help others. I think I accomplished both."

Reputation

"Reputation is a great asset in any business, but especially in real estate. There was a saying, I believe it was in Century 21 training, that 'a referred is a preferred'. They already know your reputation and there's some trust or they wouldn't refer you if they did not trust. Reputation is also essential in being able to have people need you who already trust you because their friend, their mother, or their sister told them that you're trustworthy. I've benefitted from that and I'm so thankful for it."

Customer Service

"Knowing what the customer really wants is helpful, and getting that knowledge in the beginning helps me as an agent to be able to remind them later on. 'Remember, you said you really don't want a house with old fireplaces, that you're afraid something could happen with the chimney. You don't want a basement that doesn't have daylight'. Usually, people appreciate it and they feel like at least they were heard. It makes them feel valued, and even if they decided to get a house which has something they didn't want, they appreciated that I had listened to them.

"Exceed their expectation. One way that I would sometimes do that is on their moving day. I would show up and surprise them with maybe a cooler of water and soft drinks, a bag of chips, or a bucket of chicken. People really did appreciate that because moving is stressful, and it's a lot of labor. It's a lot of work, but at the same time, it's exciting for people, especially if they're moving into their first home. Sometimes second, third, and fourth-time movers are equally excited. It sends a message that you didn't just sell them and move on. You're still treating them well.

"Other times, I've helped them to pick up. The rule of thumb was that the seller should leave the house in broom-clean condition. That was the language. People did not always do that. So, I helped to sweep the floor, pick up trash in the yard, or in some cases I have helped pay somebody to help them clean it up if a big mess was left there. I made sure that my clients knew when trash pick-up day was and that they had the correct contact information for all the utilities. I paid special attention to the clients who were moving here from out of town because it is frustrating to not know which utility company to call."

Investing in Real Estate
"Real estate is the safest investment in the world."

Work
"Work hard, work extra hours, or an extra part-time job especially when you're young and trying to acquire that first property. Set goals."

Treat Yourself Well
"'Beyond a wholesome discipline, be gentle with

yourself'. That's from the poem *Desiderata*. My greatest challenge in life, so far, has been making peace with myself. Do it. Convince yourself that you are worthy of effort, grace, and, yes, success. My second greatest life challenge was parenting. Approach parenting humbly and with tender kindness."

Think Long Term

"Think about what a single-family home in your town might sell for twenty years hence."

Race and Racism

At a Howard University graduation, General Colin Powell made the following statement, as quoted in *An American Journey*: "African Americans have come too far and we have too far yet to go to take a detour into the swamp of hatred."

"I did not feel inferior, and I was not going to let anybody make me believe I was. I was not going to allow someone else's feelings about me to become my feelings about myself. Racism was not just a black problem. It was America's problem." *My American Journey* by General Colin Powell.

Eleanor Roosevelt said, "No one can make you feel inferior without your consent."

"Racism is real, racism harms, racism hurts," says Jannie. "That said, I choose to focus on kind and decent people. I choose to work at becoming the best version of myself. I try to avoid thinking of what a racist person might think of me. It is important that we continue to advocate for laws that create a level playing field for all Americans."

"Race is a mythical line created and promoted by some people in order to enhance their profits. Racism is present in some people. Don't allow racism to stifle you. Don't harm yourself. Don't let it define you, don't let it confine you, let it refine you, energize you, to be the best possible person you can be, the best version of yourself. That is what I tried to do. It dawned on me one day that the stock market didn't know I was black. If I could get a little money mixed in with other people's money, they could not discriminate against my little money. So, I started to invest in the stock market."

"The existence of any pure race with special endowments is a myth, as is the belief that there are races all whose members are foredoomed to eternal inferiority." Franz Boas, the *Instant Quotation Dictionary*.

"A heavy guilt rests upon us for what the whites of all nations have done to the colored peoples. When we do good to them, it is not benevolence – it is atonement." Albert Schweitzer, the *Instant Quotation Dictionary*.

"I have one criticism about the Negro troops who fought under my command in the Korean War: they didn't send me enough of them." General Douglas MacArthur, the *Instant Quotation Dictionary*.

"At the heart of racism is the religious assertion that God made a creative mistake when He brought some people into being." Friedrich Otto Hertz, the *Instant Quotation Dictionary*.

"In a word, the Negro youth starts out with the presumption against him. That's from *Up From Slavery* by Booker T. Washington. What strikes me about this quote is that it was first published in 1901 and it still rings true today."

God
"I am not a person who promotes organized religion. However, I do believe there is a higher being. We can get help and guidance and instruction from that source. It's as the poem, *Desiderata*, says: 'Be at peace with God, whatever you perceive Him to be.' For me, God is love. So, I believe that I have been helped divinely, not because I sat in church every

Sunday (because I didn't) but because I tried to treat people right."

Religion

"My subconscious mind is God's cell phone to me. We connect in the early morning when my mind is uncluttered."

"As a child I was rejected by organized religion. The church left me, but God never left me. I don't think my mistakes caused God to turn on me. 'For man looketh on the outward appearance, but the Lord looketh on the heart'. That's from the Bible, 1st Samuel 16:7. That verse helped me deal with this rejection."

"Do unto others as you would have them do unto you." The Golden Rule, from the Bible.

"Love your neighbor as yourself."

Wisdom

This quote sums up the essence of my message in this book: "Thrift and toil and saving are the highways to new hopes and new possibilities." From *The Souls of Black Folk* by W.E.B. Du Bois.

"Be not afraid of going slowly, be afraid of only

standing still."
A Chinese proverb.

"Many people crucify themselves between two thieves, regret for the past and fear of the future." Les Brown, a motivational speaker.

"A fool and his money will soon part ways." "That's a saying that one of my friends accredited to her father."

"My Mom used to say, 'If everyone does a little bit, nobody gets hurt.' I used this a lot with my children. They still tease me about that."

"Nothing can bring you peace but yourself." Ralph Waldo Emerson.

"You can victimize yourself by wallowing around in your own past." Wayne Dyer, a self-help author and motivational speaker.

"Kindness is a language which the blind can see and the deaf can hear." An African proverb.

Epilogue

I did not move forward toward my goals until I learned to love and rely on myself.

With humility and gratitude I realized my goals of maintaining a healthy body weight, acquiring financial independence and helping my parents. Two habits helped me maintain a healthy weight – regular exercise (which includes yoga) and my daily weigh in. I begin each day by hopping on bathroom scales; I jot my weight in my Day-Timer. Because I note my weight each day, I know when I should pass on that second piece of chocolate cake. I learned from a public health course that "What gets measured gets done." I formed these habits decades ago and they are still serving me well.

I shared many joyous years with my parents. My siblings and I paid off our parents' farming debt in 1987. We gave them wedding anniversary celebrations, vacations, cars, and other gifts. My siblings and I celebrated every major holiday with our parents. My eternal thanks to Mom and Dad for consistently encouraging me and making it possible for me to pursue the life I now enjoy. Mom, thanks for writing every poem and short play we performed in church. Thanks, Dad for being our rock, our provider, our protector.

Thanks Lucille and Geraldine for sharing your first teaching salaries with all of the family to lift us out of poverty. Your unselfish gifts convinced our Dad that Mom was right – formal education was well worth the effort. Lucille and Gerald, largely due to your advocacy, the road we grew up on was renamed in 2018 from Old Cemetery Road to Rev. William Carter Sr. Road. Special thanks to Lucille for insisting that I graduate from college and for introducing me to the game of Bridge.

Alline, thanks for welcoming me into your home when I was homeless. My first year of college would not have been attainable (at that time) without you. Thanks also for tutoring me in Spanish and challenging me at Scrabble.

Willie Mae, thanks for allowing me to sing off key. I can still hear your melodious alto voice camouflaging my singing deficits. You were a wonderful majorette in the Halls Consolidated band.

Thanks, Rose Marie for protecting me. At age four when I awakened during the night terrified of the darkness, you were always there to turn on the light and tell me there was no need to be afraid. As we grew older, you turned on lights in my mind. Thanks for every light you have turned on for me throughout my life – especially for convincing me that I could pass the real estate exam.

William Junior and Dennis Charles, I shall never forget how you put the chalkboard in the basement at 3213 Hummingbird Drive and taught me things I should have known. You tutored me yet never made me feel inferior. Thanks for telling me that any man should be happy to be my spouse. Thanks for being my playmates and cheerleaders.

Cleo, your playful disposition often brightened up my mood. Thanks for being one of my first real estate clients. You taught me everything I know about baseball and many things about tennis and golf. Thanks for being you.

Kenneth Bernard, thank you for listening to my deepest thoughts and feelings and responding in a non-judgmental manner. I enjoy our long conversations that sometimes start with silly jokes and expand into serious philosophical debates. You are skillful at initiating a lively conversation.

Lisa, without your permission, I would not have told this story. Thanks for being my dearest advisor. It brings me joy to witness your real estate career. Jamie, thanks to you and Lisa for helping me prepare for the Graduate Record Exam. The two of you made me a stronger person. Thanks, Lisa and Jamie, for loving me in spite of my imperfect parenting efforts.

Jacob, my grandson, I feel your love. I hope you feel that same love from me in return. Being a grandparent is one of life's bonuses. Education is a necessity; decide to love learning. As you mature, think for yourself. Be the best person you can be. Our parents loved us enough to challenge us to be our best selves.

As I exit this writing, please allow me to share my idealistic vision for us, people of color. Imagine for a moment us living together in a tight knit community of love, peace, scholarly pursuits, healthy habits, neatness, cleanliness, respect for each other – a community enriched with great music and art with no illegal drug use and no violence. Some blacks have described to me feeling this sense of a safe shared community when visiting Martha's Vineyard during August. If we could create such a community, the entire world population would want to be our next-door neighbor.

My hope is that my story will inspire others to hang on to hope and pursue their goals. Family love was my salvation.

"The truth – that love is the ultimate and the highest goal to which man can aspire." Man's Search For Meaning, by Viktor E. Frankl.

Namaste

Jannie Carter Williams, 2022.
Photo by Steve Herlihy Photography.

Contact Jannie
jannie.williams@comcast.net

CPSIA information can be obtained
at www.ICGtesting.com
Printed in the USA
LVHW070053021122
732128LV00004B/5